Breathe in God's Love and Light

By
WALTER BECKLEY

BREATHE IN GOD'S LOVE AND LIGHT AND MANIFEST YOUR DREAMS

BY WALTER BECKLEY

BREATHE IN GOD'S LOVE AND LIGHT AND MANIFEST YOUR DREAMS

BY WALTER BECKLEY

Copyright © 2012 Walter Beckley

All rights reserved. This book or any portion thereof may not be reproduced or used in any manner whatsoever without the express written permission of the author except for the use of brief quotations in a book review.

Printed in the United States of America
First Printing, 2012
ISBN: 978-0-9725337-6-8

BREATHE IN GOD'S LOVE AND LIGHT AND MANIFEST YOUR DREAMS

BY **WALTER BECKLEY**

DEDICATION

With all my love I dedicate this book to
my wonderful parents.
John and Erma Jean Beckley

Your son,
Walter L. Beckley

BREATHE IN GOD'S LOVE AND LIGHT AND MANIFEST YOUR DREAMS

BY WALTER BECKLEY

Contents

DEDICATION 5
FORWARD.. 11
EDITORS OVERVIEW 13
ACKNOWLEDGMENTS 16
INTRODUCTION 19

CHAPTER 1... 27
MY PERSONAL JOURNEY 28
    MY EARLY EXPERIENCES AND PERSONAL SPIRITUAL DEVELOPMENT 30
    WHY I AM SO GRATEFUL 32

CHAPTER 2... 39
GOD'S DIVINE LOVE AND LIGHT 40
    GOD'S FINGER PRINT............................... 41
    OPENING TO THE BEAUTY OF YOU......... 41
    ACTIVATE GOD'S LOVE AND LIGHT 44

CHAPTER 3... 51
    THE SECRET 56
    OVERCOMING NEGATIVE INTENTIONS ... 58
    THE GLORIOUS HEALING POWER OF GOD'S LOVE AND LIGHT 60
    IMPROVE THE QUALITY OF YOUR LIFE 65
    STOP ABSORBING NEGATIVE BELIEFS 66
    DESPERATION VERSUS EASE 68
    BROADCASTER AND RECEIVER 68

CHAPTER 4... 71
    THE SUBCONSCIOUS IS ALL-POWERFUL.. 76
    DOES EGO MAKE IT HAPPEN? 80
    THE POWER OF ONENESS 82
    ACTIVATING THE DIVINE POWER 85
    HOW CAN I ACTIVATE MY HEALING POWER? 85
    BALANCING THE FIGHT OR FLIGHT RESPONSE.. 86
    ENTERING THE STILLNESS OF THE SUBCONSCIOUS MIND 88

BREATHE IN GOD'S LOVE AND LIGHT AND MANIFEST YOUR DREAMS

BY WALTER BECKLEY

CHAPTER 5 91
BALANCING STRESS AND NEGATIVITY 92
    WHAT IS STRESS? 93
    WHAT IS PAIN? 94
    THE IMPORTANCE OF BALANCING YOUR EMOTIONS 98

CHAPTER 6 103
THE CREATOR'S ENERGY 104
    YIN AND YANG 108
    YIN 109
    YANG 109

CHAPTER 7 113
AWARENESS, CONSCIOUSNESS & ENERGY CENTERS . 114
    7 STATES OF CONSCIOUSNESS 116
    SPIRITUAL CENTERS 122
    ESSENCE OR POWER ACTIVATED 122
    BODY LOCATION 122

CHAPTER 8 127
BREATHING IN GOD BREATHING IN FULFILLMENT 128
    WATCHING YOUR BODY BREATHE 131
    THE IMPORTANCE OF THE BREATH 132
    MANIFESTING YOUR DREAMS 136

CHAPTER 9 141
    THE FOCUS POWER BREATHING METHOD 143
    INTERNAL AND EXTERNAL EXERCISES ... 147
    THE LOCATION OF YOUR SOURCE CENTER 151
    OCEAN BREATHING MUSIC 157
    LESSON 1 – FOCUS POWER BREATHING METHOD INSTRUCTIONS 158
    RESTING PHASE 159
    FOCUS POWER BREATHING BALANCING THE INHALE AND EXHALE Advanced Level 1 162
    FOCUS POWER BREATHING DEEP ACTIVATION METHOD Advanced Level 2 164

CONCLUSION 192
ABOUT THE AUTHOR 195
    CLASSES, PRODUCTS, AND CONTACT 196

Welcome And Thanks For Reading My New Book

www.GodsLoveandLight.com/higherlearning

BREATHE IN GOD'S LOVE AND LIGHT AND MANIFEST YOUR DREAMS

BY WALTER BECKLEY

BREATHE IN GOD'S LOVE AND LIGHT AND MANIFEST YOUR DREAMS

BY WALTER BECKLEY

FORWARD

As I write this forward, I find myself having two reactions. First, I am proud to write this forward for my brother and support him in his work. Secondly, I am impressed with the volume of knowledge and expertise my brother expresses in this newest book from his background and experience.

Breathe in God's Love and Light, is the first of Walter's books that I have read and I found it to be surprising, thought provoking and compassionate.

Surprising, because as one who had a level of skepticism, as Walter mentions in the book, I was surprised as my skepticism was calmly erased as I read the motive and insight that was revealed from the heart of the author and his vast experience. As stated on page 19, these concepts are radical to a degree, but I also see how they can change one's life. Walter has invested much time and energy, and a great deal of heart and passion into learning these concepts for himself, and more importantly into sharing them. As you read these ideas, I encourage you to think of them as thoughts to help deepen the foundation of your current path and experiences.

Thought provoking, because these concepts make you think and rethink the foundation of your belief system, to ensure that where you stand, begins with a firm foundation in God and who God is to you. As Walter states, the book is not intended to take the place of the religious belief system that you have, but it will help you clarify whether your belief system is stable enough to allow you to become all that God has created you to be.

Compassionate, because it expresses the author's heart for people to know God and achieve the level of existence that God has created for them.

I am proud of the work that Walter has done to bring the information to the forefront of our minds; to give us the opportunity to experience the fullness of our creation as God's creatures; and to experience all that God would have us to experience in our lives.

As you read, be prepared to learn, evaluate and grow into all that God would have you to be.

Joshua Beckley
BA., MA., Ph.D.
Redlands, CA. 92373

BREATHE IN GOD'S LOVE AND LIGHT AND MANIFEST YOUR DREAMS

BY WALTER BECKLEY

EDITORS OVERVIEW

Breathe in God's Love and Light and Manifest Your Dreams offers brilliant insight into the components that make us fully human yet uniquely divine. Through it we learn and are reminded that we are special and unique creatures, created in God's image with unlimited potential for greatness. However, many of us are full of blockages and hindrances that keep us from moving forward in our lives – these due to trauma, abuses, disappointments and failures that we've experienced. Walter Beckley helps the reader to identify these negative root issues that cause us pain and turmoil and begin to address and heal the underlying issues that inhibit our growth.

Walter explains through very practical, simple, yet profound teachings and insights how negative thought patterns are stored in our subconscious minds and block and inhibit the flow of God's Love and Light in our lives. These negative emotions and mental attitudes also cause physical illness, pain and Dis-ease that we might not be aware as having spiritual or emotional root causes.
Through his experience and expertise in various philosophical disciplines, Mr. Beckley is able to provide insight into the whys and hows of human behavior and psychology and how we can overcome these negative thought patterns by welcoming the presence of God into our lives.

The concepts in Breathe in God's love and Light are not meant as a replacement to what you already believe but an enhancement. As spiritual people we are encouraged to spend time with God, in the quiet and stillness of His presence.

BREATHE IN GOD'S LOVE AND LIGHT AND MANIFEST YOUR DREAMS

BY WALTER BECKLEY

Breathe in God's Love and Light simply provides a tool and a discipline for how to focus ourselves while we're there.

Princess Parker
Chief Editor, Start to Finish Publishing
Evanston, IL

YOU ARE GOD'S LOVE AND LIGHT

BREATHE IN GOD'S LOVE AND LIGHT AND MANIFEST YOUR DREAMS

BY WALTER BECKLEY

ACKNOWLEDGMENTS

I would like to thank the many teachers, religious ministers, energy workers, and spiritual healers with whom I have been involved over the years. Through discipline and God's Love and Light, these men and women have instructed me in various spiritual principles: how to heal and awaken, and how to get more out of life. I would also like to acknowledge these wonderful workers for the heart-felt love and devotion they have shared, in order to assist mankind in the progression toward greater good in life.

A special thanks goes to my good friend, student, and brother Marty Doyle. I am very thankful that you have been an instrumental part in the creation of God's work. Our talks about life, people, finances, and more, gave impetus to my writing and communicating about awakening God's Love and Light. Although the world needs more Marty Doyles, I am honored that I have the one and only as my friend.

BREATHE IN GOD'S LOVE AND LIGHT AND MANIFEST YOUR DREAMS

BY WALTER BECKLEY

SPECIAL THANKS TO SO MANY WONDERFUL SUPPORTERS

I'd also like to thank my many helpers, helpmates and supporters for being so consistent through the years in standing with me and sharing in this work. Your assistance has been a gift and a blessing.

Many thanks go out to: John Weston, Madeline Goldstein, John Butler, Marty Doyle, Dr. Deidre Burrell, Dr. Jifunza and Fred Wright, Luvina McCray, Tammie Watson, Mantak Chia, John Weston, Chike Akua, JR Fenwick, Isaac Portilla, Roslyn Renee Commodore, and, to all of you who are not listed, please forgive me for not including your names. I do thank you from my heart to yours.

I would also like to acknowledge my grandson Kaeleb Hayes for the wonderful pictures that he took; thank you Kaeleb for being my photographer.

I also would like offer a very special thanks to my first and second editor's Robin Pundzak, and Princess Parker. Thank you, Princess for your commitment and for your vast knowledge and insight.

Cheers to Radiant Living Publishing and to our new publishing company "Start To Finish Publishing" whose mission is to assist aspiring writers in reaching their goals in audio, video and print.

"www.StartToFinishPublishing.com"

| BREATHE IN GOD'S LOVE AND LIGHT AND MANIFEST YOUR DREAMS | BY WALTER BECKLEY |

UNLOCK THE ABILITY OF LOVE IN YOUR LIFE!

BREATHE IN GOD'S LOVE AND LIGHT AND MANIFEST YOUR DREAMS

BY WALTER BECKLEY

INTRODUCTION

What if there was a way that you could make your life exactly the way you wanted it to be? What if, despite what is going on in the world's economy, your personal finances could flourish? What if you could find a way to release the negativity that has been implanted within, causing polarized, limited thinking processes, painfully destructive emotional upheavals, and excessive physical deterioration which impede your capacity to flourish in life?

Our spiritualized human potential has yet to be maximized. Our Creator has instilled in us the potential of unlimited creativity and possibilities. You are the spiritualized potential of God; your essence, when aligned with the Creator, unlocks the magnificence of your being. The beauty of all this is that we're just getting started.

The information in this book is radical; it will change your life. Some may see this work, these concepts and ideas as limited; others may view it as complex and even a little frightening - especially if you compare it to the fundamentals of a religious life. This book is not meant to take the place of the religious belief system that you've already adopted in your life, giving you safety and security between you and God.

BREATHE IN GOD'S LOVE AND LIGHT AND MANIFEST YOUR DREAMS

BY WALTER BECKLEY

One of my reasons for sharing this information is based on the lives I have seen changed for the better throughout my 25 plus years as a teacher, trainer, life coach, and energetic healer. I feel extremely blessed for my personal relationship with God's Love and Light and the ability to share this experience with others. Everyone who has come to me sincerely seeking to learn this system has gained some measure of change, greater insight and or felt some degree of God's grace. Many have released a measure of the pain or weight that was stopping them from achieving success in life. This work is about what flows through me and what God is able to do, not just through me, but in you.

It is important that you get this! My greatest wish is that you will find an inner and outer connection with God's Love and Light. I hope that you cultivate a beautiful relationship and your life becomes everything you've ever wanted.

BREATHE IN GOD'S LOVE AND LIGHT AND MANIFEST YOUR DREAMS

BY WALTER BECKLEY

MY MISSION

As the founder of The School of Radiant Living, my mission has been to serve people. The school's personal development systems and training methods help you understand the fundamental principles of energy and how they can affect your life. The various methods we offer, enable you to connect, cultivate, and direct your life force. You develop higher levels of functioning and balance, empowering the physical, mental, and emotional phases of your life.

Since 1989 I have enjoyed sharing various ideas and methods for activating a deeper relationship with God. Through the years of teaching at the School of Radiant Living, I have systematically utilized this inner power of God's Love and Light to attract that which is needed for greater prosperity and spiritual growth. The power of the simple methods outlined in these pages is expansive. They offer greater levels of awakening healing, and the manifestation of material gains. The systems outlined in this book have been tried and tested thousands of times with great success. For the first time, there is a systematic way to undo the negative programming that stress, trauma, and negative thinking have over your life.

BREATHE IN GOD'S LOVE AND LIGHT AND MANIFEST YOUR DREAMS

BY WALTER BECKLEY

THE EXPERIENCE

Throughout the years I have had many personal experiences that have deepened my spiritual growth and understanding. The opportunity of working with thousands of students, clients, family, and friends has resulted in a unique sharing of information and feedback. This information has helped me develop a simple and powerful way to connect with God's Love and Light. Accessing this presence enables one to overcome the many obstacles stressors, and traumatic experiences that block success. I have seen and I have felt the energy at work in my own life, as well as in the lives of my many students and now you will too.

No matter what else I say or write, this is of utmost importance - God's Love and Light is within you! Like a gold miner mining for gold, your job or goal in life is to mine for God's Love and Light in your life. Much like a blazing sun, cultivate the radiance of God's essence deep into your very being. Don't stop until the Creator's radiance shines through you, awakening a new you, reborn with the freshness of constantly living in awe of the beauty and abundance of what God's Love and Light offers.

BREATHE IN GOD'S LOVE AND LIGHT AND MANIFEST YOUR DREAMS

BY WALTER BECKLEY

Some very simple but profound tools will enable you to go further in every aspect of your life. The reason they work is based on the biblical verse which states, "But seek ye first the kingdom of God, and his righteousness; and all these things shall be added unto you." (Mathew 6:33)

Proper understanding of God's Love and Light is not based on logic, but on experience. This is why Psalm 46:10 states, "Be still, and know that I am God". This verse goes even further to say what will happen when you do become still, "I will be exalted among the nations, I will be exalted in the earth." By becoming still, your experience of just who God is expands and changes in your life.

Unfortunately, most people have no idea or concept of how to be still, even though most of the universe is built upon stillness. In learning to be still, you are also learning to be without form - stilling your mind from all thoughts, conceptions, and ideas. You are also learning to still your emotions from the ebb and flow of feelings and actions. When all actions stop and you become still, you are ready, an empty vessel to be filled with God's Love and Light.

BREATHE IN GOD'S LOVE AND LIGHT AND MANIFEST YOUR DREAMS

BY WALTER BECKLEY

THE SYSTEM

You are a spark of God's Love and Light – You will learn through the Focus Power Personal Development System to access your inner flame, changing your life to a fulfilled experience of radiant energy. The system is based on the principles of meditation, focused breathing, and specific exercises. It is a simple but highly effective way to awaken and unite body, mind, and spirit, based on the flow of Love and Light into your body and life.

Science has discovered that all of life is made of energy. There are negative energies and positive energies. These energies affect your health, your ability to gain or access wealth, as well as the quality of your relationships and the world around you. Your body is also energy; your mind uses subtle pathways to communicate with your body and the world through energy. However, your body's network of computer-like communication is vastly superior and light years beyond what our scientists can even imagine.

With practice, you will learn to create and enhance the endurance necessary in your body, mind, and energy field. You will be able to access and hold the frequency of God's essence for longer and longer periods of time. This work will enable you to become a clearer and stronger vessel for

BREATHE IN GOD'S LOVE AND LIGHT AND MANIFEST YOUR DREAMS

BY WALTER BECKLEY

the Creator's will. The outpouring of God's purpose will manifest through you into creation.

We are capable of living a long and beautifully fulfilling life. However, in order for the truth to be unveiled, we must learn the beauty of letting go, returning to stillness, and receiving the power of love.

As you learn to cultivate your relationship within, there are several steps that will gently unveil themselves to you:

- As you become full of God's Love and Light, you become healthier, empowered and more deeply in love with all of life.

- As you learn and follow our unique step-by-step breathing system, you will be cultivating the healing power within.

- You'll also learn to activate your inner vision, which gives you greater clarity and focus.

- You will learn how to tap into and unleash your inner power for greater success in manifesting your dreams

BREATHE IN GOD'S LOVE AND LIGHT AND MANIFEST YOUR DREAMS

BY WALTER BECKLEY

I will show you various concepts and ideas of how God's Love and Light can work in your life. As you continue your journey into this powerful relationship, you will experience a richer, more loving way to be in life. You will awaken to your higher purpose in life and find lasting fulfillment.

CHAPTER 1

BREATHE IN GOD'S LOVE AND LIGHT AND MANIFEST YOUR DREAMS

BY WALTER BECKLEY

MY PERSONAL JOURNEY

In 1977 I embarked upon a journey, seeking to improve the state of my mind, body, emotions, and spiritual relationship with God. I learned, while being on this new path, that the overall quality of my life was in God's hands. I met many people who led me through wonderful and enlightening experiences, as well some that were not so good. The experiences challenged me to seek and discover the inner truth of God's Love and Light, giving it mastery over my life. I know now that everything was sacred food for my life's journey. God placed everyone and everything in my life as guide posts, signs, and messages. The obstacles, stress, and trauma, negative and positive experiences served as training on every level. Everything was set up by the unseen hand of the author of my life, the author of all life and eternity.

Through the years, I have met and studied with many remarkable people, some in the United States and others abroad. I have learned from spiritual healers, religious teachers, scientists, meta-physicians, and energy workers. I have been taught by many master teachers of yoga, meditation, chi kung, massage, and tai chi. Combined, these dedicated people through the years have instructed

BREATHE IN GOD'S LOVE AND LIGHT AND MANIFEST YOUR DREAMS

BY WALTER BECKLEY

me in understanding how to heal, awaken, and spiritually develop. Most of the wonderful people that I met were on

the path of awakening their minds, bodies and spirits to their highest potential. A small percentage of these instructors that I met were already fully-realized spiritual beings, living and basking in God's eternal grace.

After 13 years of mind, body, energy, and spiritual training, I began to teach others. In 1989, I became a certified Healing Way Energy instructor; I taught and assisted others in their awakening and healing process. However, after years of working one-on-one, in small groups, and with large organizations, I found myself challenged by my students' growth. I decided to let go of various commitments and move deeper into my personal and spiritual development. It was time for me to go within, simplify, and bring out the essence of these teachings. I wanted to make the way easier and less mysterious.

MY EARLY EXPERIENCES AND PERSONAL SPIRITUAL DEVELOPMENT

My spiritual training started when I was very young. I remember being four or five years old, sitting on my bed meditating. Of course I didn't know what I was doing at the time. Later, I realized that by just sitting and being still, I would have some really nice experiences; I enjoyed the connection I was having.

Later on, I began to understand the art of meditation. I had an intense desire to awaken my inner spirit. When I was going through the Church and being baptized, I knew that my lights were all going to be turned on. I would be able to experience a higher level of enlightenment. Although I am appreciative of my earlier religious training in the church, I knew I wanted something more. As I look back, I wonder how I knew so much about being enlightened at that age. I must have been born with that awareness.

When I was about sixteen or seventeen years of age, I began to hunger for an even deeper relationship with God. I would read the Bible because that was the only book, of which I knew, that talked about the Spirit of God. I would study over and over, reading verses about my relationship with the Holy Spirit. As I studied, quiet and alone,

BREATHE IN GOD'S LOVE AND LIGHT AND MANIFEST YOUR DREAMS

BY WALTER BECKLEY

something would kick-in which I can only refer to as an anointing. This anointing of God's Love and Light opened up a deeper knowledge; an understanding of my life in relationship with God. In the midst of being still, I would become full and awakened with this understanding about my spirit, about my soul, and about my connection with God, Jesus (The Christ Consciousness), and the Holy Spirit. In that instant I knew, on every level of my being, that everyone had this power of God within them.

With this new revelation came a need for more. I needed to focus, to contemplate, to find a peaceful place inside myself. Thank God one of my older cousins, who is a black belt in karate, had just learned how to meditate. He shared with me some of what he knew, and I began to practice. I went upstairs, sat down on my bedroom floor, closed my eyes, and focused as he had told me. It was strong enough to draw me right to my inner source of stillness; in about 30 seconds I went right in and I knew that I was no longer just my body. There was a part of me that was greater than all the space that filled the room, the entire outdoors, and all space and time. I knew, in that instance, that I was part of the great I AM. I thank my cousin, Early Colman, for being my first informal meditation teacher.

BREATHE IN GOD'S LOVE AND LIGHT AND MANIFEST YOUR DREAMS

BY WALTER BECKLEY

WHY I AM SO GRATEFUL

My personal relationship with God has assisted me in my spiritual, mental, physical, and emotional understanding, clearing and awakening me to my higher Spiritual Self. While delving deeper into my own personal and spiritual development, I was forced to examine the teachings and training that I offered to my many students through the years. It was time for me to re-examine all that I had learned and had been teaching.

I discovered another level of understanding, which was more profound than I could ever have imagined. This new level of experience brought it all together. Previously, I had practiced various forms of breath work. However, after returning from India in 1995 it became clear, the power of life and death were tied to the power within the breath. By learning to gently cultivate the breath in the right way, you begin to increase the body's capacity for God's Love and Light to increase in your body and in your life. To make this method even more effective, I created a simple but high powered musical cadence to help with the rhythm of the breath. I called this method and the music "Ocean Breathing."

After years of success with teaching and assisting others in their health, healing, and spiritual growth, another level of

BREATHE IN GOD'S LOVE AND LIGHT AND MANIFEST YOUR DREAMS

BY WALTER BECKLEY

expression unveiled itself. It had been sitting there patiently waiting. You have this next level in your hands, as you read these pages and learn to experience God's Love and Light.

BREATHE IN GOD'S LOVE AND LIGHT AND MANIFEST YOUR DREAMS

BY WALTER BECKLEY

HISTORICAL PROSPECTIVE OF MY TRAINING

This is a short overview of just a few of the many systems and methods I have studied through the years. In 1977 I discovered Transcendental Meditation. One of the most appealing aspects about Transcendental Meditation (TM) is the hundreds of published research studies that have been done and continue to be done on the mind, body and the various levels of consciousness. This research about the power of individual and collective consciousness is worth taking the time to read.

In April of 1978, I received my second certificate of completion from Joliet Junior College on the studies of the mind, "Advanced Self-Hypnosis". This was revolutionary at the time and introduced me to the concept of "auras," the body's visual and kinesthetic energy fields. I also was schooled in the ideas of positive versus negative thinking, galvanic skin response sensors, and galvanic measurement devices.

I began learning how to access divine healing power in the winter of 1982 by studying Siddha Yoga meditation. Siddha Yoga is a very old system of meditation and yoga. It is a system that is passed from a master teacher to a disciple or a dedicated student, who has surrendered to God. At that time, Swami Muktananda, the founder of Siddha

Yoga, had a meditation center in upper state New York. I would often journey to New York for meditation intensives. Meditation intensives are sessions devoted to awakening the light of God into your life.

In the fall of 1988, I was introduced to the Healing Tao system by Taoist Grand Master Mantak Chia. Mantak Chia's work enabled me to clearly see things that had previously been shrouded in mystery and esoteric language. For the first time, I truly understood the internal purpose of the work I had done for the past 11 years. I recognized the various stages of energy at work in the physical, mental, and emotional aspect of my existence.

More importantly, I learned that there were steps one can take to personally understand, activate and cultivate the various forms of energy into daily life. In 1989 I was certified to teach the Healing Tao system, which is now called the Universal Healing Tao System. I went on to be certified in several other energy healing methods from various Master teachers and novices from around the world.

BREATHE IN GOD'S LOVE AND LIGHT AND MANIFEST YOUR DREAMS

BY WALTER BECKLEY

I am very thankful that in the midst of my own personal growth and challenges, I discovered these vital teachings. This transformative information enabled me to release my

own self-imposed layers of negative emotional energies. I freed myself from various forms of pain, stuck mindsets and other negative energetic connections. Ultimately, I was able to navigate through my personal transformation and into the next level of spiritual growth and understanding.

As I move forward each and every moment, I am constantly being reassured from within. I know that I can let go and advance in my life; the beauty and power I once thought I would find outside of myself and in the world, is nestled close within me.

BREATHE IN GOD'S LOVE AND LIGHT AND MANIFEST YOUR DREAMS

BY WALTER BECKLEY

THE SPARK OF GOD'S LIFE WITHIN

There is nothing more precious than the spark of life that is within each of us. All of creation has manifested from this spark and nothing escapes its grasp. The spark of life has been called many things: the Holy Spirit, Kundalini, the breath of life, Ki, chi, Serpentine Fire, and others. It has been witnessed in prayer and meditation, in a healing, when a child is born, or in the death experience.

You can cultivate this spark to become your conscience state of awareness. It can manifest and witness all that you experience. The spark of life enables a person to experience the world from the eyes of the Divine, to hear the sounds of the Divine, to enjoy the smells of the Divine, and the tastes of the Divine.

You are no stranger to this Divine experience of life; you have only forgotten who you really truly are. This is definitely not a mystery. You only have to learn how to cultivate the life that is already within you.

Cultivating the life inside you begins with providing for your body. Plants provide food for the body; various herbs provide healing for the body; water hydrates and quenches the thirst of a body; and fresh air enlivens the body. When you provide the best nourishment for the body, along with consciously connecting how you breathe to the essence within the breath, you awaken the pure awareness or consciousness of the Spirit of God, which dwells within the body as Love and Light more easily. This nourishment of the body enables it to handle the vibration, frequency, strength and power of God's Love and Light.

It is extremely important to develop the inner strength to take refuge in God's power within. You can then learn to expand God's Essence outside of yourself and into all of your relationships throughout life.

CHAPTER 2

BREATHE IN GOD'S LOVE AND LIGHT AND MANIFEST YOUR DREAMS

BY WALTER BECKLEY

GOD'S DIVINE LOVE AND LIGHT

When Love fills the heart,

The mind becomes still,

When the heart is filled with Love,

The mind is illumined,

When the heart is filled with Love,

You're guided by Divine Will,

When the heart overflows with Love,

Right and wrong,

Good or bad,

Black and white,

All opposites become broken,

And everything dissolves into oneness

When the heart is filled and overflows with God's Divine Love,

Divisions release, and merge into the oneness of God's Love and Light.

For a greater experience in life,

It's time to Learn to be in harmony with God's Love and Light,

Breathe in God's Love and Light all the time,

Become empowered and be in love with life,

Like never before!

- Walter Beckley

BREATHE IN GOD'S LOVE AND LIGHT AND MANIFEST YOUR DREAMS

BY WALTER BECKLEY

GOD'S FINGER PRINT

Our Creator's fingerprint has been left on the manifestation called creation. God marked creation with the glory and Essence of the Holy Spirit, which we experience as Love and Light. There is no place that you can go, nothing that you can touch, no part of the earth or universe that does not contain God's fingerprint. God's magnificence has been written upon your heart and delivered unto you through the power and beauty of breath. That breath is the breath of life, which made you a living soul. Breathing in the breath of God's Love and Light enables you to tap into all of God's blessings. These blessings can take many forms that we may have never before considered.

OPENING TO THE BEAUTY OF YOU

Are you open to learning about your own healing power? Are you open to understanding and experiencing the magnitude of power that lies within you? Opening to the beauty within you leads to creativity and the unbounded opulence of love, joy, and happiness. Are you ready for greater health, wealth, and success in life? Are you ready to start constructively designing the life that you desire, from the inside out? Well, it is my honor to share this information. I have watched thousands of people get what

BREATHE IN GOD'S LOVE AND LIGHT AND MANIFEST YOUR DREAMS

BY WALTER BECKLEY

they want out of life when they turn within, to the power of Love and Light.

Most of our lives, we have been taught that what we want is outside of ourselves. This type of thinking leads to a false focus. We connect with a false belief that power is outside of us; that true power is about having external gains. Don't get me wrong, there is nothing wrong with having material success in life. However, you should first focus on the power that is within you, rather than seeing your prosperity or power as something coming from outside of yourself.

Many people look at their house, their car, their spouse, and other material gains as the source of their happiness. Once we learn to connect from the inside out, we realize that the true manifesting power and creative source is within. It is the same source from which all things flow. This ocean of unlimited manifesting power is within you; it is the sheer beauty and power of God's Love and Light. In order to fully realize the common relationship between you and all objects, you must recognize and experience your inner life force. The power that is within you is the same power that is within all things. You are in relationship with all of life, and all of life is in relationship

BREATHE IN GOD'S LOVE AND LIGHT AND MANIFEST YOUR DREAMS

BY WALTER BECKLEY

with you. Therefore, when you develop the ability to connect with your inner source of power, all that you need will manifest unto you through God's divine grace, which is connected to all of life.

GOD'S DIVINE HEALING POWER

Many people already realize that their life is a series of events moving them into a direct relationship with God. However, they don't understand that the relationship is already available, within this present moment, with God's creative Essence. Because you are alive, you are a product and expansion of God's Love and Light; it radiates through you as you!

I know that many of you, like I, have encountered a boatload of negative experiences in life. These physical, mental, and emotional issues cause turmoil and strife. That negativity can very often paint a very different picture of life; making you doubt how much of God's Love and Light is available to you. You are probably very skeptical, and this is okay. I want you to be skeptical. However, being skeptical is not the same as being closed. If you are skeptical, you can still see or experience what I will share. I want you to keep your belief system. The only thing that I am sharing with you is a deeper experience of

God's grace. Until you learn to experience the full essence of God's power, I want you to be skeptical. When you have the experience, then you will know. Then you can share the experience!

ACTIVATE GOD'S LOVE AND LIGHT

God's Love and Light radiates through all of creation, including the negative and positive energies of life. If you awaken and operate in conjunction with that power, you learn what divine beauty, grace, compassion, and joy really offer.

1 John 1:5 (NKJV) This is the message which we have heard from Him and declare to you, that God is light and in Him is no darkness at all.

Your life is very similar to a battery. A battery is strong in the beginning; it is vibrant and capable of driving or operating a device. However, with constant use it soon runs out of energy. If the battery is not connected with a source of power that can recharge it, then the device will start to falter. It won't operate correctly, and the battery will die.

Like the battery, when your energy is high you operate more efficiently in life, and in a more positive way. When

BREATHE IN GOD'S LOVE AND LIGHT AND MANIFEST YOUR DREAMS

BY WALTER BECKLEY

your energy is low, you become inefficient. With low energy, your body and mind cannot operate correctly, your emotions are irritated and you don't have the power

and the much-needed strength to overcome challenges. Activating God's Love and Light will recharge your energy levels and make positive changes in your life.

So supercharge your life now! If people have water in their gas tank, it isn't any wonder why their car runs so sluggishly. Similarly, if you have negative energy inside, you should not wonder why your life runs so sluggishly, with challenge after challenge. We all know that high-octane gas makes the car engine run more efficiently. When you release your negative emotional energy and learn to connect with the high octane God power, your life will run more efficiently. Love and Light is the energy - the power you were meant to experience. If you want to become a winner at life's race, run with the Creator's power; the power of God's Love and Light.

I realize that many of you may have never felt your own divine healing power before. Using the exercises in the following chapters, you will easily connect with and experience the energy that flows through you. Don't worry about doing everything perfectly or having a perfect experience right away. Everyone can learn to experience and cultivate this relationship more fully and completely over time.

Awakening the true power of loving and nurturing relationships is the ultimate expression of God's Love and Light. You don't need to look very far to understand the power of love. Think of the innocence and beauty of a newborn baby which can enthrall people, captivate their hearts and moves their minds. The connection we feel with this new infant touches something deep within. When we see a newborn baby, we recognize the possibilities and power of this new outpouring of life. We understand, on a deeper level, how this precious gift of life connects with the Creator's Love and Light.

The relationship between the mother, father, and their newborn baby reaches deep within the parents; it touches the very essence of their being. This connection is almost unexplainable, however once established, the parents will sacrifice their life for their newborn child. This invisible connection establishes a very unique bond based on protecting the life force within the child.

BREATHE IN GOD'S LOVE AND LIGHT AND MANIFEST YOUR DREAMS

BY WALTER BECKLEY

The level of joy that the mother and father have for their newborn is magnified 100 trillion times and more by the Creator, when it comes to what God sees and feels for you. Our loving relationships allow us to ride the common thread of God's Love and Light. All of our experiences in

life, whether negative or positive, have God's essence at their foundation. Everything has been built on the Creator's power and love.

This common thread of relationships can be compared to water. There are many different types of water, such as salt water, freshwater, or muddy water. There are also many different types of relationships. You can choose positive relationships, negative relationships, loving relationships, and friendly relationships. In the water analogy, you may say that H^2O is the common thread. In relationships, God's Love and Light is the common thread.

When we awaken to this level of awareness many people have a deep sense of completeness, but not in the sense of being "done." We are speaking of a completeness that enters us into the continuum of everlasting life. This is a level of self-awareness in which your feelings and experiences are in a state of dynamic satisfaction.

BREATHE IN GOD'S LOVE AND LIGHT AND MANIFEST YOUR DREAMS

BY WALTER BECKLEY

When your spiritual radiance and vibrancy is expressed at the highest level throughout your body, your life will be transformed. Your body is the vehicle, or container, for the expression of God's will. When you are aligned with God's Love and Light, your body will share and exude the

beauty, bliss, and magnificence of this quality of life with others. God has given mankind the ability to experience God's unlimited power of creation and love. Completeness, balance, and harmony are just a few of the spiritual attributes given to us through the Creator's spiritual essence. When we drop down deep within ourselves, we begin to recognize our source and experience our infinite nature. When you begin to see and experience this, you will become struck by the beauty and simplicity of the power stored within each of us

Enjoyment is one of the fruits of life. You were designed to be filled with God's Love and Light, which is bliss and eternal happiness. In order to experience your reservoir of bliss, you must learn to release your negative blocking energies. This will enhance your creative, free flowing energies in order to balance and maximize your life's potential.

BREATHE IN GOD'S LOVE AND LIGHT AND MANIFEST YOUR DREAMS

BY WALTER BECKLEY

Our Focus Power Personal Development System is very different; probably unlike anything you have done or tried up to this point. However, it is important that you do something different in order to obtain a different result. It is said that insanity is when you do the same thing over and over again, expecting a different result. When you

learn to cultivate your divine breath, you will not be doing the same thing. The Focus Power Personal Development System enables you to tap into the everlasting fountain of the divine essence of God. You will enhance your creativity and manifest your dreams, unleashing them through you and into the world.

In this way, we become co-creators with God's unbounded source of divine power. Your reservoir of Love and Light, which is the divine source of God, offers you total freedom of expression. Simply by learning to breathe with the Focus Power Breathing Method, you will tap into and connect with your inner source of unlimited creative bliss, which is your true source of happiness.

BREATHE IN GOD'S LOVE AND LIGHT AND MANIFEST YOUR DREAMS

BY WALTER BECKLEY

1 John 4:7-8 *⁷ Beloved, let us love one another, for love is of God; and everyone who loves is born of God and knows God. ⁸ He who does not love does not know God, for God is love.*

Chapter 3

BREATHE IN GOD'S LOVE AND LIGHT AND MANIFEST YOUR DREAMS

BY WALTER BECKLEY

DISCOVERING AND EMPOWERING YOUR GIFT WITHIN

Many people have a negative mindset. They believe in what will not happen as opposed to what can happen. They believe in what will not work instead of looking at the possibilities that are available. When doubt and consistent negative intentions become your illusionary master, then negative energy and force will support your negative expectations. They will become your reality.

PLANTING POSITIVE SEEDS IN THE GARDEN OF YOUR MIND

Positive thinking is so important. Imagine how good you would feel if you constantly and consistently planted the seeds of love, virtue, righteousness, and all other positive ideas. The seeds of joy, happiness and all good experiences would become a part of your life. You and only you, in your divinely creative relationship with the Creator, can activate all that you ask for and seek in life. It is important that you become proactive. Ask for, think of, sense, and feel the goodness and sweetness that life has to offer.

It is time to wake up, to the true concepts and ideals that you want in your life. It is also important that you release thinking about what is not possible. Always focus on the

BREATHE IN GOD'S LOVE AND LIGHT AND MANIFEST YOUR DREAMS

BY WALTER BECKLEY

possibility of what you want. Allow good thoughts regarding what you want in life to float around and grow inside of you. Possibilities and divine opportunities are waiting for you. It is time for you to receive and experience the magnificent power and beauty of God's Love and Light. It is manifesting completeness so that you can live your life in a most glorious and wonderful fashion at all times. It is important that you realize this truth. Negative beliefs, lack of faith, and negative thoughts or actions can have you stuck in a more negative experience or view of life.

It is important to learn to uncover negative beliefs, and reinstall new positive beliefs that support your goals in life. Don't worry about what is going on around you. It is more important that you cultivate how and what you really feel inside your body – your mind and emotional connections. Converse with and listen to what's really inside your inner garden of life (your mind and emotions). Once you enter into this sacred place, be still and experience the sunshine of God's Love and the illumination of God's Light. Inside of this wonderful relationship, see your heart and your life standing and bathing in the sunshine of love, joy, and happiness. With this new awareness as a reality, imagine, feel and experience how powerful and enriched your life experience will be.

BREATHE IN GOD'S LOVE AND LIGHT AND MANIFEST YOUR DREAMS

BY WALTER BECKLEY

Discover, uncover, recover, and nurture the gift that you are. During each and every waking moment, we have the ability to access the sheer splendor and beauty of being a spiritual creator. However, we are living in a society that cultivates negative energy in every possible way.

If there was ever a time that we needed God's Love and Light in our lives, it is now! This is a time of much hatred, famine, suffering, poverty, and disease. There is so much negative emotional energy available, that we could destroy one another 7 times over and still not be satisfied. We're in total opposition to positive life force; we choose destruction. Most people choose to walk on and over other people in order to get what they want in life.

When people are asked what they want out of life, they will talk about things like, money, power, sex, fame, relationships and possessions. Yes, people want to be happy, but they believe it is the money and or the things that they can acquire that will make them happy. It is my sincere hope that I will shine a small light that grows into a blazing flame, dispelling the illusions of where true joy is found. It is my prayer that this flame awakens each of us, moving us forward in truth, empowered by the Creator's everlasting Love and Light.

BREATHE IN GOD'S LOVE AND LIGHT AND MANIFEST YOUR DREAMS

BY WALTER BECKLEY

There are various concepts that enable God's Love and Light to work in your life. You can activate a deeper relationship that overcomes various physical, mental, emotional, as well as material challenges that may have created perceived barriers in your life.

As you continue your journey into this powerful relationship you will experience three powerful attributes:

- A deeply richer, more loving way to be in life
- An awakening to your higher purpose in life
- Lasting fulfillment

BREATHE IN GOD'S LOVE AND LIGHT AND MANIFEST YOUR DREAMS

BY WALTER BECKLEY

THE SECRET

Positive thinking and positive thoughts are the seed ideas that you must plant in the garden of your life. Like a good farmer, you cultivate your seeds daily by watering, or affirming your seed thoughts and ideas. Next, you give them plenty of sunshine by placing them in God's Divine Love and Light. Your seed ideas will become nourished and bear the fruit that you have desired. The Creator's good energy is designed to help you manifest your life. You will grow physically, mentally, emotionally, and spiritually as well as manifest warm, genuine relationships with family, friends, and all of life.

However, not many people know how positive thinking works. They want things, but they don't believe that they are deserving of them. So instead, they speak against the very things they really want. This is how people enter into negative, rather than positive thinking. The greatest downside of negative thinking is that it takes away from the building energy that the Creator has in store for you. Within the destructive walls of negative thinking, you have less energy. The energy is stuck, caught up, or being diverted into debilitating mental agitation and confusion.

BREATHE IN GOD'S LOVE AND LIGHT AND MANIFEST YOUR DREAMS

BY WALTER BECKLEY

When the seeds of negativity have produced weeds throughout your garden, choking off the positive loving

forces designed for your life, you feel unworthy or argumentative. You have to fight through life instead of enjoy life. If you're feeling less creative and more destructive, positive ideas have difficulty growing.

BREATHE IN GOD'S LOVE AND LIGHT AND MANIFEST YOUR DREAMS

BY WALTER BECKLEY

OVERCOMING NEGATIVE INTENTIONS

It is very important to understand the principle of magnetism. Many people don't realize how energy and magnetic forces of attraction and repulsion work. A magnet has 2 sides - a positive side and a negative side. The positive side of the magnet has the ability to attract its opposite, or that which is desired. The negative side of the magnet has the ability to repulse, or push away, that which is undesired. It is also important to understand that both sides of the magnet have the ability to attract or repulse. Much like the polarity of a magnet, within us we have energy which attracts and repulses. This energy is invisible, but it can be felt. We attract some things into our lives and repulse or push away others. We may be conscious or unconscious of what it is that we are attracting or repulsing.

In the same way, based on our experiences, we have created and aligned various energies with negative and positive forces. This connection of our internal energies with magnetic forces brings us consistently to that which is most dominant. So if anger and frustration are more dominant than harmony and integration, then you will act in the power of the stronger magnetic force - anger and frustration. However, if your experiences in life connect with love, joy, and happiness, then you are magnetically drawn to Love and Light.

These laws are at work whether you are aware of them or not. The effects of these energetic and magnetic seed experiences, whether known or unknown, have been planted in the garden of your life. They are bearing or will bear the current results in your life.

There is a reason why you are not getting what you want. If you plant an apple seed, you expect to get an apple tree. Similarly, if you were to plant corn seeds, you would not expect to grow an oak tree. You and I both know that if you plant corn seeds, you should expect to receive ears of corn. Why should it be any different when you plant negative seeds in the garden of your mind? Should you not expect to receive negative results?

BREATHE IN GOD'S LOVE AND LIGHT AND MANIFEST YOUR DREAMS

BY WALTER BECKLEY

THE GLORIOUS HEALING POWER OF GOD'S LOVE AND LIGHT

I would like for you to walk with me, having an open mind. One that is full of life's most glorious, beautiful, and miraculous possibilities. During my life, I have witnessed many miraculous events and experiences. I have also witnessed thousands of miraculous events and transformations that have taken place in the lives of my students, clients, and friends. One of the most extraordinary was the healing of a friend, Artemia, whom surgeons and doctors said was beyond hope. This experience deepened my faith, in what the power of God's Love and Light can do, especially when it comes to our assistance in the healing process of another person.

On February 13, 2009, Artemia suffered a massive brain aneurysm. Paramedics brought her to the hospital around 12:30 in the afternoon, but it was 8:30 that evening before the surgeon arrived. She drifted into a deep coma and bled for eight hours before she was seen by the surgeon. Her first surgery was to release the pressure from the bleeding. Then surgeons underwent a second surgery to find the source of the rupture; it was unsuccessful.

BREATHE IN GOD'S LOVE AND LIGHT AND MANIFEST YOUR DREAMS

BY WALTER BECKLEY

The next day, Artemia was resting with her family and friends all around her. The doctor came in to check her vitals in the hope that somehow the bleeding would stop and heal on its own. Later that evening, while her eyes were still closed, Artemia sat straight up in bed, with all of the life-support equipment still connected to her body. The nurses tried to get her to lie back down, but that is the point where I believe that her bleeding started again and she entered into a full coma.

The next day when the doctor came in to see her, he tapped her eyes with a piece of paper. When she did not blink, the surgeon immediately realized that her state had deteriorated. He promptly started emergency procedures and took her back into surgery for the third time, trying to find the true source of her bleed. After four or five hours of surgery, he was successful at stopping the bleeding..

She then endured several weeks of life support, with a tracheal tube in her throat for breathing and a peg in her stomach for feeding. Artemia was unresponsive and in a coma. The neurologist stated that her brainstem had shut down, and there was no brain function.

BREATHE IN GOD'S LOVE AND LIGHT AND MANIFEST YOUR DREAMS

BY WALTER BECKLEY

The family's options were bleak. One of the options was to pull the plug from her life-support. The other option was to open the top of her head and cut out part of her brain.

That would release the pressure from swelling and relieve her pain. Fortunately, the family decided against both of those options.

Up to this point, I had been following the doctors. I was quiet because I felt that it was not my domain. I had been scanning her body energetically and communicating with the Love and Light that was within her. But that day something rose up inside of me and told me to go to work; told me to start doing more of what I inwardly knew I should do.

After several weeks of working on her, passing God's Love and Light into her body, a new awareness started percolating inside of me. I needed to increase the Love and Light by getting more people to help jumpstart her body. I asked Artemia's son, Ryan, and sister, Gina, if they would help me to increase the love light energy. They both immediately agreed. I immediately began to charge their bodies with power, simply by touching their hands and passing energy from my palm points to theirs. When they

BREATHE IN GOD'S LOVE AND LIGHT AND MANIFEST YOUR DREAMS

BY WALTER BECKLEY

could feel the energy, they told me so; Ryan then held her ankles, to help ground the energy. Gina stood on the heart side, holding her left hand and sending energy into her body. I was on her right side, holding her right hand,

sending Love and Light into her body. I told Gina and Ryan to picture the life force flowing through them; to allow his Love and Light to flow into Artemia.

Within a few minutes, Artemia started to respond. She started twitching, and then she let her legs up, moving them for the first time. This was the beginning of the larger movements that would continue to take place, as Artemia began to reoccupy her body.

I continued to work with Artemia for about another 45 days, until she was able to walk out of the hospital with a walker. Over the course of the next month, I worked with her until she could leave the walker alone. Almost 4 years have passed, and every now and then I'll hear from Artemia. Although the doctor wrote a book about her surgical miracle, she never lets me forget. She thanks me, for she knows that this is work that came through me from our Creator. God's power of Love and Light assisted her in her time of need. I did nothing; the power of Love and Light that flows through me did it all.

I tell this story to illustrate not only the healing power of God's grace, but also the difference that positive energy can make in your life. Positive energy comes from positive

thinking. It comes from the seed ideas that you plant in the garden of your life. Those ideas can lead to significant improvements in the quality of your life.

IMPROVE THE QUALITY OF YOUR LIFE

This book is filled with strategies that will improve the quality of your life. No matter what is going on in your life at this point, you can achieve a higher level. You can attain a greater experience of freedom; you can attract wealth, opulence, money, health, and wonderful relationships.

In order to improve the quality of your life, learn to be still and feel good about this present moment and experience. Absorb the warm and very gentle awareness of being loved by God.

You don't understand truly how unlimited you are. Most people create limits around various aspects of their lives. It is your responsibility to remove the limits from your life. It is your responsibility to cultivate and experience the greatest life possible, no matter what you may have suffered in the past. It is time to stop sending negative emotional energy out into the world. Stop planting more seeds calling forth more negative experiences. As you sow, so shall you reap!

BREATHE IN GOD'S LOVE AND LIGHT AND MANIFEST YOUR DREAMS

BY WALTER BECKLEY

STOP ABSORBING NEGATIVE BELIEFS

It's time to stop absorbing the negative beliefs of others - friends, the government, school systems, and even religions. Don't accept, until you first question, how these beliefs may be affecting and or destroying your life. There is good in religion, there is good in the school system, there is good in the government, and there is good in your family and friends. What I want you to be aware of is that all of those good systems and people in your life also have negative understandings. Those negative beliefs do not promote you and what you're trying to welcome into your life. You **CANNOT** have more than you ever believed possible. It's like trying to go forward, when you don't take your foot off the brake.

Your thoughts trigger feelings within your body, which create other thoughts, which create deeper feelings. If your thoughts are negative they will create negative feelings in your body. Your body will release hormones, which will create other feelings. Those feelings attract more negative thoughts in your mind, which will create deeper negative feelings. An ongoing cycle is created. Part of your work, is to remove the limits that you placed upon yourself, and grow the abundance of your life. This universe is vast; your ability is unlimited. When we learn

BREATHE IN GOD'S LOVE AND LIGHT AND MANIFEST YOUR DREAMS

BY WALTER BECKLEY

to mix the right elements together, we begin to manifest that which we seek. Just like making a great cake, we must recognize the materials that are needed. The Creator has already supplied all the ingredients that we will need. The next step is to mix together the ingredients in the right proportions.

The first ingredient is your will. If your will is weak, it will not hold together or formulate that which you seek to manifest. When making a cake, if you add a teaspoon of flour and a gallon of water, will it become a cake? No, all of the necessary ingredients for making a cake are not present. This is an example of weak will. Sometimes when wanting to manifest that which we desire, we do not have all of the components available, and in the right amounts. Our anger or fear, etc... is more dominate than our courage or joy.

If your will is too strong, it can break the mixing bowl. In other words, all of the components may be destroyed before you can formulate that which you seek to manifest. When we look at a lily, we recognize that its complexity is sheer genius. It expresses the masterfulness of the Creator's will and ability to manifest.

BREATHE IN GOD'S LOVE AND LIGHT AND MANIFEST YOUR DREAMS

BY WALTER BECKLEY

DESPERATION VERSUS EASE

You can have anything that you want in life, as long as you don't need it. The feelings that you get when you need something, activates and draws upon the negative energy of desperation.[1] The energy of immediate desperation attracts more desperation, which creates more anxiety, bringing forth even more desperation. Desperation brings forth more desperation, just as anger brings forth more anger. The good news is that love will bring forth more love, joy will bring forth more joy, and harmonious feelings will bring about a deeper sense of harmony. When you desire to have something more added to your life, become happy and more loving; make sure that you are being easy. Don't be weak like a noodle; become firm, yet gentle and kind - to yourself and to everyone else.

BROADCASTER AND RECEIVER

Like a radio station that you dial into, you can dial into the frequencies of life that give you exactly what you need to receive. If there was just one frequency that you were dialing into at any given moment, it would be easy.

---

[1] This is my interpretation of some information I received from Dr. Joe Vitale, connected with my experience with God's Love and Light. I love how Dr. Joe puts it, plus I have watched these laws at work in my life, and it will offer a magnificent awakening for those of you who apply this information to their life.

However, it is not just one frequency that is at work in your life. You are constantly being bombarded with hundreds, if not thousands, of various frequencies, which

create negative and positive feelings and thoughts in your life. Many of those feelings and thoughts you are aware of, and many you are not.

Your goal is to harmonize and neutralize these various negative and positive feeling or frequencies into Love and Light. You will begin this transformational and forgiveness process as you learn the Focus Power Personal Development System.

BREATHE IN GOD'S LOVE AND LIGHT AND MANIFEST YOUR DREAMS

BY
WALTER BECKLEY

CHAPTER 4

BREATHE IN GOD'S LOVE AND LIGHT AND MANIFEST YOUR DREAMS

BY WALTER BECKLEY

AWAKENING YOUR BEAUTIFUL MIND

There is a uniqueness of spirit within you that is unparalleled throughout all of creation. When awakened, that spirit is found to be immutable, omniscient, and unfathomable. Yet, at the same time, it is sublime, tender, loving, and full of joy. As much as I try, these descriptions pale in comparison to the truth of your spirit. The uniqueness and beauty of what dwells within you is truly breathtaking.

The ancients were often known as seers, yogis, monks, and prophets. They were the indwellers of the inner planes of the mind, body, and spirit. They saw, experienced and became the breath of God's Love and Light. They would write down and share their experiences verbally, discussing the power and beauty of God's grace. They came to these realizations through deep prayer, meditation, contemplation, and breath work. They learned to understand the power of the mind by activating God's Love and Light and cultivating a relationship that erased, transformed and forgave them of their current state of heart and mind. Through God's Love they would heal and open their hearts and God's Light would illumine their minds from their unenlightened sick self.

Proverbs 4:23, Keep thy heart with all diligence; for out of it [are] the issues of life. (KJV)

BREATHE IN GOD'S LOVE AND LIGHT AND MANIFEST YOUR DREAMS

BY WALTER BECKLEY

Proverbs 4:23, *Guard your heart more than anything else, because the source of your life flows from it.* (GWT)

THE POWER OF YOUR MIND

Your mind is the director; the key to overcoming your body's physical pains and emotional imbalances. It is your mind which has witnessed all forms of abuse and affliction. It is your mind which will command and take your body through the rigors of releasing deep-seated negative emotional energies. It will be through the development and/or freeing of your mind that you can move into the purification and stillness of God's Love and Light. Take care of your mind; learn to develop the mind beyond thinking, right and wrong actions, and into stillness.

This is why the mind rules, for without it, how can you find the way? How can you become ready for being one with God's grace?

CONSCIOUS MIND VERSUS SUBCONSCIOUS MIND

There is a division within you, and this division is based on the two aspects of your mind. You have a conscious mind and a subconscious mind.

BREATHE IN GOD'S LOVE AND LIGHT AND MANIFEST YOUR DREAMS

BY WALTER BECKLEY

CONSCIOUS MIND

Your conscious mind, is constantly at work making decisions based on logic and reasoning. The conscious mind controls the actions that you make based on purposeful actions. For instance, you may make an intentional decision to go to work or call a loved one. Moving your fingers or toes, and eating a banana are all choices made by your conscious mind.

SUBCONSCIOUS MIND

The subconscious mind is the part of your mind that is responsible for all of your involuntary actions. Your heart rate, breathing, digestion, kidney and organ functions are just some of the many actions controlled by your subconscious mind.

When you have an experience, it leaves a residue on your screen of consciousness; it becomes embedded into the subconscious. Some of this residue we recognize and it is connected to our memory. Other bits of this residue we recognize as feelings or emotions. Our conscious memory and our subconscious memory work together, filtering our current moment of reality with our past experiences.

BREATHE IN GOD'S LOVE AND LIGHT AND MANIFEST YOUR DREAMS

BY WALTER BECKLEY

When we see a loved one, our conscious memory recognizes them. Our subconscious memory immediately starts filtering through and checking on various feelings that we may have experienced with our loved one. This filter enables us to remember the good or bad feelings that we have regarding this person. All of our limitations about being with this person, become activated. For instance when you return home for Thanksgiving to see your loved ones, you are subconsciously reconnected to that environment.

That is why people experience some of the most emotional upheavals at family get-togethers. They say and do things in response to past events that they thought they had gotten over. They eat foods that they normally would not eat. These are responses to memories dredged up by the subconscious. Often these reactions are out of character, like becoming more lively and outrageous, or shy and shut down. It is the actions of the subconscious mind that may stop you from getting the better job or make you say things you would not normally say - they call them Freudian slips.

THE SUBCONSCIOUS IS ALL-POWERFUL

Our emotions carry electromagnetic and chemically activated charges. For instance, when someone becomes angry, the electromagnetic charges that surround past experiences of being angry combine together. This charge moves through the emotional energy system activating the organs and glands, causing the release of chemicals and hormones. This results in an even more hyper-response of negative emotions within the body regarding the current given experience. A host of other experiences of anger come together for the protection or destruction of the individual.

Your subconscious mind also controls your emotions. This is why you may often feel anger, fear, worry, anxiety or sadness without wanting to experience these or any other type of negative feeling. Deep within the subconscious mind is the storage place for your beliefs and memories, both old and new. Your subconscious is your foundation; it ties your conscious experience of life to the old negative thoughts, patterns, and experiences. This is why change is so difficult. Your conscious mind is trying to change negative patterns and is meeting resistance because of your subconscious mind.

BREATHE IN GOD'S LOVE AND LIGHT AND MANIFEST YOUR DREAMS

BY WALTER BECKLEY

It is said that the greatest battle in life is not the war outside of you, but the opponent within. This is where the battle between the two minds is held; war is waged and you become your own victim or victor. The conscious mind states what it wants, while the subconscious mind begins to manifest what you really believe from deep within your body's organs and glands, where you have stored your past negative and positive experiences. Your organs and glands act like storage bins, housing both your positive and negative emotional energies. They also act like broadcasting stations and radio receivers, drawing in and expressing the various forms of like energy. These invisible forms of energy can be experienced as vibrations and frequencies, which then affect the organs and glands. We recognize this combination of energetic variations as feelings. It is very important to understand that you may be holding in more negative energy than positive energy, despite what you may be thinking. This is why you may say or desire one thing, and yet manifest something different.

On the next two pages, the charts are designed to show the various organs and how they act as broadcasting stations and like radio receivers. Below each organ you will see the type of programming energy with which it is aligned and sends out and receives.

BREATHE IN GOD'S LOVE AND LIGHT AND MANIFEST YOUR DREAMS

BY WALTER BECKLEY

SUBCONSCIOUS NEGATIVE EMOTIONAL STORAGE BINS

KIDNEYS	LIVER	HEART	SPLEEN	LUNGS
Fear	Anger	Arrogance	Worry	Sadness
Paralysis	Rage	Hastiness	Concern	Grief
Weakness	Bitterness	Cruelty	Being Closed	Avoidance
	Hostility	Abandonment		

1. Ref: Mantak Chia's Book "Transforming Stress Into Vitality"

BREATHE IN GOD'S LOVE AND LIGHT AND MANIFEST YOUR DREAMS

BY WALTER BECKLEY

SUBCONSCIOUS
POSITIVE EMOTIONAL STORAGE BINS

KIDNEYS	LIVER	HEART	SPLEEN	LUNGS
Gentleness	Friendliness	Love	Openness	Courage
Softness	Comfort	Joy	Fairness	Righteousness
Safety	Kindness	Happiness	Unselfishness	Strength

BREATHE IN GOD'S LOVE AND LIGHT AND MANIFEST YOUR DREAMS

BY WALTER BECKLEY

WHAT PART OF THE MIND IS IN CONTROL?

Your conscious mind has entered into perpetual conflict with the subconscious mind. Your conscious mind goes through life like a hamster on a wheel. Your conscious mind may think it's in control, but it's not; herein lies the conflict of your life.

Within the subconscious mind lies vast potential for greatness. However within the subconscious mind, man is in constant flux between negativity and positivity, past versus present, and illusions versus truth. When there is no balance, the lines of division can create conflict. In essence, the subconscious mind perceives all experiences as if they just happened or are happening. While the conscious mind has difficulty staying fully illuminated in this present moment. When we learn to illuminate the conscious and sub-conscious mind God's Love and Light balances all dualities.

DOES EGO MAKE IT HAPPEN?

Egotistically, we may feel a sense of power and control when we seemingly take things into our own hands. Sometimes people fight over very important issues, and sometimes very mundane ones. We have even formed

BREATHE IN GOD'S LOVE AND LIGHT AND MANIFEST YOUR DREAMS

BY WALTER BECKLEY

debate teams, which is a nice term to use for arguing the issue.

There is a space, a place, an experience beyond the ego. This field of pure bliss is within you and extends into infinity. When you learn to practice gratefulness rather than indulging the ego, your world will change. It is so important to understand this next statement, for it will change your life. The world around you reacts to God's Love and Light. It is the ultimate form of communication. This is the source of your life, and it has been acting on your behalf since before you came into being.

For the individual who experiences God's true Love and Light, being grateful is a heartfelt experience. God's love is the grace in life, the oil that loosens the gears of negativity. When this starts to happen in your life, gracefulness becomes a natural byproduct. You can jumpstart God's grace by learning to be grateful in each and every moment; even while being wronged, be thankful for the breath of life that flows from your nostrils.

It is God's power which flows through your nostrils when you breathe. When cultivated, you will find peace beyond measure, joy here and now, and discover the sweet

BREATHE IN GOD'S LOVE AND LIGHT AND MANIFEST YOUR DREAMS

BY WALTER BECKLEY

pleasure of having a heart filled with God's love and your mind illuminated with God's light.

THE POWER OF ONENESS

Understanding the concept of Oneness will help you develop faster, make better choices and experience life more completely. Oneness includes the idea that we are collectively one human family; we are one with all things.

Oneness also applies to the interconnections within our bodies. Although seemingly independent, the various functions of the body are not separate. This means our organs and glands, hormones, emotions, and psychological functions are synergistically operating together - harmoniously, as one integrated life.

We are not separate. The ideas or actions that lead to separation, bring about division, division brings on variations, these variations - bring about imbalance, and imbalance leads to disharmony. The ideal experience of life is to be in harmony or oneness - internally in the body and externally in the world.

Many people see the problems of the world, as problems outside of themselves. And there are those people who

BREATHE IN GOD'S LOVE AND LIGHT AND MANIFEST YOUR DREAMS

BY WALTER BECKLEY

see the problems within their body, as separate from or disconnected from the world. Can man affect the world? And is it not true that man has had an effect on the world? Can the world affect man? And has the world had an effect on man? Both man and the world have been beautiful, creative, and destructive.

When we look at the elemental constructs of man and the earth, it is important to understand that love and joy, as well as destruction and illusions are a part of the vibratory choices we can make. Both disharmonious vibrations and harmonious vibrations are available. These vibrations are both energetic and invisible; however, they can be seen through the inner eye and physical eyes when the hypothalamus and pituitary glands are illumined. When activated, the clean and vibrant energies of God's Love and Light flow through the body very easily, creating positive harmonious qualities.

Negative qualities incite disharmony and block the flow of God's life force. Negative energies can create abrasive residue, agitation in the body, imbalances in the emotions, as-well-as diminish the clarity of the mind.

Your mind is the gatekeeper that tries to decide what positive or negative energies are allowed into your body. Once those energies are either repulsed or allowed inside, they become vibrations (or frequencies); your internal organs and glands express the vibrations as feelings. In turn, the feelings affect the actions and interactions of a person. It is important to recognize that these feelings, which have their root within frequencies and vibrations, flow through the organs and glands. They activate various reactions and counter-reactions inside the body's chemistry. These reactions are projected as emotions or feelings, connected with words, expressions, and actions. It is important to understand which organs and glands are connected with which emotional response.

There are five major organs and glands which govern the various emotional responses. These major organs and glands generate both negative and positive emotions.

BREATHE IN GOD'S LOVE AND LIGHT AND MANIFEST YOUR DREAMS

BY WALTER BECKLEY

ACTIVATING THE DIVINE POWER

Physical struggles in your body are often caused by agitations in your mind, and negative emotional energies. These energies are generated by various experiences you have had in your life. Your inner grace transforms the negativity into usable energy. God's Divine Love and Light evaporate these contaminants from your body; the healing essence of divine healing power is in your breath. When we learn to breathe in God's Love and Light we automatically receive the divine healing essence over our lives.

HOW CAN I ACTIVATE MY HEALING POWER?

As I have mentioned throughout this book, the healing power is within you. The easiest way to locate this inner source of power is through your "navel center." The navel center is the space about 1 to 3 inches below your navel. The navel center will vary slightly from person to person. When you learn to connect with your navel center, through focused breathing, you will start to actively connect with your inner healing source of power. You will learn to gently allow and guide your breath inward and deeper into your internal source; your mind, breath and energy will sink down inside of you, with softness and gentleness into your navel center. Once you find this inner softness and inner glow, you will begin to cultivate a heart-felt connection with God's healing power. In turn, God's divine essence will begin to connect with you. If you pursue it, then Love and Light will pursue you (you take one step and God takes two). Learn to sit, become still, and do nothing; continue to breathe, watch your breath, until you let go and it takes off.

Love and Light is designed to overrule your sick self. As your heart radiates with the power of love, your mind becomes illumined with the thought of love. Over time, your heart stands in a continuous and harmonious relationship with your breath. As this happens, you will experience the fact that God's divine healing power of Love and Light is within. That fact will help you to deal with stress and the effects that stress has on your body.

BALANCING THE FIGHT OR FLIGHT RESPONSE

How you respond to a stressful challenge will depend upon the type of stress you encounter. Whenever you are faced with a stressful challenge there is a physiological effect on your body. Your nervous system activates hormones which cause you to react to the threat, in order to protect yourself. This reaction enables you to get away or run away, as fast as you can. This is a part of the fight or flight response; it is your sympathetic nervous system reacting to a stressful situation.

During these times the body produces extra chemicals such as adrenaline, cortisol, and non-adrenaline, which increase alertness, raise the heart rate, initiate rapid breathing, increase muscle preparedness and blood flow. These are some of the changes that the body goes through when preparing to meet the challenge and to protect itself.

In contrast, other body functions slowdown in order to meet the emergency. The digestive system and other nonessential functions slow down so that vital resources may be used by other systems in order to handle the stressful situation.

Factors other than threat or emergency can also cause stress. Sickness and trauma are often at the root of a person's stress levels. What is trauma? Trauma can be a physical, emotional, or mental response to a terrible event. The typical aftereffects of trauma are denial, shock, and confusion. Severe trauma can also result in long term consequences.

BREATHE IN GOD'S LOVE AND LIGHT AND MANIFEST YOUR DREAMS

BY WALTER BECKLEY

ENTERING THE STILLNESS OF THE SUBCONSCIOUS MIND

"Be still, and know that I am God" (Psalm 46:10)
This verse is a winner's verse. To win at life, you have to have the right stuff; to make a good cake you have to have the right ingredients. Stillness is the right ingredient for understanding and experiencing God's bountiful power of Love and Light. All of life is based upon the foundation of stillness. This is why the Creator says, "Be still, and know that I am God."

When you learn to become still, your conscious mind, with all of its limiting clamoring, shuts up. Your conscious mind begins to marvel at the beauty and power that it discovers within stillness. When you become still, your subconscious mind can start releasing the negativity that it has been holding onto. Your subconscious mind has cloaked all of your unresolved issues so that you might function in life, bearing all of your chaos. As you become still, your subconscious and conscious minds begin to balance and heal.

As you learn to focus your mind through The Focus Power Personal Development System, you begin the forgiveness process of transforming your negative emotions and experiences into God's Love and Light. When people go through this process, they often have flashes of past experiences. I refer to this process as downloading. Downloading is a way for the body to release the stress and negative emotions it has encountered.

Your subconscious mind can be accessed through the voice and the breath. The key to utilizing the voice and breath is through their alignment with the inner voice and inner breath. Controlled focused breathing will activate the inner breath, slowing down your body and mind. Over time, your body will become still.

CHAPTER 5

BALANCING STRESS AND NEGATIVITY

Emotional imbalances occur when a person has an overwhelming sense of stress or psychological trauma, which challenges their ability to cope with life effectively. It is important to balance these emotions to avoid further problems, and usually this balance requires dealing with negative emotions.

Negative emotions are feelings which have imbalanced characteristics or negative charges. They can often lead to self-defeating attitudes, and a gradual decline in the normal thinking process. Frequently, negative emotions gain power leading towards depression and even suicidal thoughts, because of a person's self-defeating attitude about life. Over long periods of time, continuous negative emotions can change or even pervert a person's entire personality. Negative emotions can cause debilitating feelings that lead to a circular chain reaction; they can cause self-destructive behavior, which impact personal health, causing further deterioration, leading toward more negative emotional feelings.

An imbalance of emotions in the body can also include an excess of positive emotions. Like negative emotions, they also can cause debilitating feelings or self-destructive behavior. Sometimes too much of a good thing can be bad.

Certain things like over-enthusiasm or extreme forms of elation and passion can activate excessive positive emotions which can lead to imbalances or false positive negative emotional feelings.

WHAT IS STRESS?

Stress is often associated with anything that poses a challenge or a threat to our well-being causing various degrees of physical, mental and or emotional pain. Today people are overloaded with stress. In the back of their minds, they wonder whether they can really cope or keep up with the pressures placed upon them every day. People are under stress from all directions. Whatever may pose a challenge or threat to your well-being is stressful. It is almost impossible to live a life without some form of stress. Some stress is good for you, like the stress that motivates you to get out of bed in the morning, in order to make things happen. Other good stress could be the stress you feel when you're picking out a gift for someone you love. Some stress will cause you to be creative; it will challenge you. However, it is the destructive or negative stress which we must learn to release or overcome. It is important to understand that some stress will assist you, while other forms of stress will destroy you.

WHAT IS PAIN?

Pain is usually an unpleasant sensation often caused by intense or damaging stimuli. The International Association for the Study of Pain has a definition that is widely used, "Pain is an unpleasant sensory and emotional experience associated with actual or potential tissue damage, or described in terms of such damage."

Pain motivates individuals to withdraw from damaging situations, to protect a damaged body part while it heals, and to avoid similar experiences in the future. Most pain promptly resolves once the painful stimulus is removed and the body has healed. Sometimes pain persists despite removal of the stimulus and apparent healing of the body; it may arise in the absence of any detectable stimulus, damage or disease.

According to Wikipedia, pain is the most common reason for physician consultation in the United States. It is a major symptom of many medical conditions, and can significantly interfere with a person's quality of life and general functioning[2].

OVERCOMING CHALLENGES, STRESS AND TRAUMA

Challenges come in many forms and serve to wear you down and pull on your energy. Day after day, your energy is being drained from you physically, mentally, and emotionally.

Rather than getting closer, the things you want to have in your life seem to sink further and further from your grasp, until another check mark for the failure side of life is etched into your sub-consciousness. You try eating the right foods, getting to sleep earlier, and thinking the right thoughts however you keep being pulled into the negativity of despair. Unfortunately, most people have never consciously activated the power within, and learned how to use that power to recharge their lives. Cultivating the Divine Power recharges your life!

This is the true source of the Power of all of life. If you feel disconnected from life or drained by stress and trauma, life becomes raggedy and not worth living. Even if your

---

[2] Wikipedia.com

BREATHE IN GOD'S LOVE AND LIGHT AND MANIFEST YOUR DREAMS

BY WALTER BECKLEY

life is not miserable, wouldn't it better if you could decrease your negative experiences and increase the love and happiness? Imagine what it would feel like to experience God's Love and Light in your life! You have a choice, and the choice is a simple one. You can continue doing exactly what you've been doing, expecting to get a different result; or your second choice, my favorite, you can develop a personal relationship with God's Divine Power.

I have watched God's essence manifest countless miracles in people's lives. I have seen such powerful and positive changes take place; I know without a shadow of a doubt that it is the unseen hand of the Lord. The grace and power of God can truly move mountains. Now I must confess, I have not seen God's Power move any mountains myself, but I have seen it move people; I have seen it remove illness; I have seen it heal relationships; and I have seen it open the door for financial freedom.

When you become more aware of the unlimited potential that the Creator has instilled in you, you awaken to a willingness to manifest; a willingness to be of service to others. Be grateful for this moment in time; cultivate a relationship with the Divine Power of God within.

BREATHE IN GOD'S LOVE AND LIGHT AND MANIFEST YOUR DREAMS

BY WALTER BECKLEY

Your clarity of this reality, of this experience in your body, is veiled by various forms of contamination. There are seven basic forms of contamination that disable the pure experience of God's Love and Light. Each of these forms of contamination keeps the individual from being inwardly still, in peace and harmony with each and every moment.

Let's explore the contaminants that block the flow of God's Love and Light in your life. In order to understand the contaminations that impede the progress of your life, it is important to understand the natural flow, and the ultimate experience that the Divine has in store for your life. Just as sunlight flows from the sun onto the earth, so also does God's Love and Light flow from the source of God into mankind.

The Seven Basic Forms of Contamination:

1. Stress
2. Trauma
3. Sickness
4. Physical Pain
5. Emotional Challenges
6. Mental Agitations
7. Lies / Fantasies / Illusions

BREATHE IN GOD'S LOVE AND LIGHT AND MANIFEST YOUR DREAMS

BY WALTER BECKLEY

THE IMPORTANCE OF BALANCING YOUR EMOTIONS

Emotional balance, leads to optimal physical health. The quality of your emotions will either weaken or strengthen your life. The divine healing power that flows in you also flows into both your negative and positive emotions. These positive and negative emotions inspire life or bring about destruction. Your feelings become vehicles for your divine essence.

The feelings that you experience are a part of the contamination that you've experienced throughout your life. The contamination is an accumulation of all unbalanced emotions. As the divine source of Love and Light seeks to express God's fullness and beauty in your life, the contamination distorts your connection, and blocks your experience. The results are unintended actions - lies that are told, lies that you receive, or contaminated information that you attract.

When we learn to breathe in Love and Light, we activate our conscious awareness of stillness, allowing the light of God to dispel the darkness within. His power transforms the expression of our physical actions, emotional feelings, and mental concepts into the harmony of Love and Light.

BREATHE IN GOD'S LOVE AND LIGHT AND MANIFEST YOUR DREAMS

BY WALTER BECKLEY

There are three identifiers that will help you empower your life. All of life is made of energy which comes from the Creator. There is positive flowing energy and there is negative flowing energy. In essence, there is energy which flows up (positive) and there is energy which flows down (negative). As with all things in life, too much of a good, or even a not so good, thing can be destructive. Your goal is to find the correct temperature for you to move through life in a healthy way.

The Three Identifiers are:

1. Identifying the problems with the **energy that flows within you**. The energy that flows within you affects your mental, emotional, and physical health.
2. Identifying the problems with the **energy that is leaving you**. The energies that flow from you affect your relationships, creativity, career, job, life style, and finances.
3. Identifying the problems with the **energy that is returning to you**. The energies that come to you affect your energy levels, sexual desires, and spiritual awareness.

BREATHE IN GOD'S LOVE AND LIGHT AND MANIFEST YOUR DREAMS

BY WALTER BECKLEY

"The Lord God formed the man from the dust of the ground and breathed into his nostrils the breath of life, and the man become a living being..."
Genesis 2:7

Ultimate Destination

Spiritual integration is a process which takes place with the divine power of God's Love and Light, which is the ultimate destination within the human experience while on earth.

A Spiritual Awakening is the result of releasing all that is inconsequential in life. Although everything matters, we must ascertain the degree of importance that actions, thoughts, and feelings have over the transformation we seek. Spiritual integration through transmutation is the ultimate result of releasing the overly stimulated active mind, unbalanced negative emotions, and stress-filled body. There are many levels of spiritual integration which will take place as you cultivate the breath of God's Love and Light in your life.

As we stated previously, it is important to have an understanding of the stages that you may experience as you breakthrough your self-defeating patterns. These destructive forms of negative internal mechanics are designed to sabotage your greatness in life.

BREATHE IN GOD'S LOVE AND LIGHT AND MANIFEST YOUR DREAMS

BY WALTER BECKLEY

When we learn to cultivate the eternal breath which is with every living person, we begin to transform our current state of consciousness into the wholeness and beauty of that which only God's Love and Light can offer.

YOU ARE A SPARK OF GOD'S LOVE AND LIGHT!

BREATHE IN GOD'S LOVE AND LIGHT AND MANIFEST YOUR DREAMS

BY WALTER BECKLEY

CHAPTER 6

BREATHE IN GOD'S LOVE AND LIGHT AND MANIFEST YOUR DREAMS

BY WALTER BECKLEY

THE CREATOR'S ENERGY

Everything is energy. When I say everything, I mean the earth is energy; your body is energy; the entire cosmos is made of energy. The ancient seers took the time to go within and experience the Love and Light of God. They recognized that the micro experiences within the body, as well as the macro experiences outside the body, are all made of energy. Whatever energy is going on outside in the world is also going on inside our body and mind.

Everything in life is made of energy. Now why is that so important? Simply because everything you want and need in life is made of energy. Einstein wrote the profound equation which also states that all of life is energy. Einstein wrote it this way:

E=MC² meaning E equals MC squared.

E equals energy

MC equals all mass and space

Mass–energy equivalence: $E = mc^2$, **energy and mass are equivalent and transmutable.**

In essence - everything is energy!

BREATHE IN GOD'S LOVE AND LIGHT AND MANIFEST YOUR DREAMS

BY WALTER BECKLEY

When we look at the big picture from the universe to atoms, everything from top to bottom is energy. That energy vibrates at various speeds and frequencies, producing everything in creation. When you have the proper equipment to look at an object, you will see that the object which appears solid is filled with holes - the solid forms are actually light and energy. Nothing is solid, although it may look, appear, and feel solid. Instead, it is a massive display of energy vibrating at a very high speed, creating a molecular structure. Science has long recognized the enormous potential within a single atom. Using the potential of a single atom, scientists created an atomic bomb. This same atomic potential is also within each of the trillions of atoms inside of you. In essence, you are more powerful than an atomic bomb. However, an atomic bomb's materials are no threat when in the hands of someone who is unaware. In the same way, you are no threat to destroying darkness when you are not actively participating and cultivating your unlimited potential. Most human beings miss the opportunity to awaken their true potential. They fail to become a powerful being, a fully humanized being of God's Love and Light. We face a dichotomy - unenlightened versus enlightened, limited versus limitlessness, impossible versus possible.

BREATHE IN GOD'S LOVE AND LIGHT AND MANIFEST YOUR DREAMS

BY WALTER BECKLEY

We are vibrational beings and ours is a vibrational universe. Many people will not accept the concept that we live in the ocean of vibrational energy. They prefer to see the world much like the ancients who thought the earth was flat and all structures were solid. However, everything that you observe and experience through your body is a matter of vibrational interpretation.

- ➤ You hear because your ears translate vibrations.
- ➤ You see because your eyes translate vibrations.
- ➤ You smell because your nose translates vibrations.
- ➤ You taste because your tongue translates vibrations.
- ➤ You feel because your skin translates vibrations.

All of our senses translate and interpret vibrations. This is how we are able to experience our environment. Because the experiences of translating vibration through our senses vary from person to person, we may have different interpretations regarding given experiences. The interpretations vary based on a person's level of conscious awareness. In essence, our physical senses do not tell us the absolute value or absolute truth about a given experience.

BREATHE IN GOD'S LOVE AND LIGHT AND MANIFEST YOUR DREAMS

BY WALTER BECKLEY

All energy emits a vibration and frequency. Our senses act as receptors that interpret the vibrations and frequencies. We are also energy and frequency generators. Based on our level of energetic flow, we broadcast negative or positive mental and emotional energy. The most potent form of energy is thought. A thought has a frequency, a biochemical and bioelectrical property, which is capable of drawing in similar energy for maximum support.

When you begin thinking a thought over and over again and imagining that thought in your mind, you are experiencing visualization. You begin drawing that concept or idea into manifestation for your life. In essence, when you imagine certain thoughts over and over in your mind, you begin broadcasting those frequencies into existence, manifesting your thoughts and feelings into your life.

To consciously manifest your will and desires, it is important to hold those thoughts and images clearly in your mind. Feel yourself embody those ideas as if they already exist. This is the philosophy behind the Chinese concept of Yin and Yang.

YIN AND YANG

Yin and Yang are two very powerful words which represent the contrasting attributes of duality and the various principles. The contrasting attributes can give rise to action, inertia, growth, destruction, friction, stillness, smoothness and harmony etc....

One of the principles of Yin and Yang states that energy is being absorbed and energy is being expanded.

One phase of energy is negative, dark, soft, yielding and feminine (Yin). The other opposite phase is positive, bright, hard, unbreakable and masculine (Yang). This is just a handful of the unlimited multitude of contrasting principles that manifest in various forms and levels of intensity. These various attributes and principles belong to the family or characteristics of Yin or Yang. Their interaction influences the destinies of all creatures and things. With proper training human beings can learn to choose which attributes they want to absorb and expand. At the zenith of human experience and potential you can absorb and expand into everything at the same time, encompassing all of creation, thereby experiencing unification with all of life and all of existence.

BREATHE IN GOD'S LOVE AND LIGHT AND MANIFEST YOUR DREAMS

BY WALTER BECKLEY

Below is a chart to assist you with what the ancients understood to demonstrate the fundamental qualities of Yin and Yang energies.

CHART OF YIN AND YANG

YIN	YANG
Negative	Positive
Soft	Hard
Night	Sunshine
Destruction	Construction
Feminine	Masculine
Female	Male
Cold	Hot
Winter	Summer
Wet	Dry
Active	Passive

Everything in the universe works rhythmically, and everything in creation works in cycles, moving in waves of pulsating and undulating energy. Light moves in waves, the heart beats in time, and the earth orbits the sun, all creating a rhythmic flow to life.

There are thousands of rhythmic movements of energy taking place within your body. These movements are called bio-rhythms. There are thousands of bio-rhythms taking place in your body, all at the same time.

YIN ABSORPTION

Yin energy absorbs. Your yin is currently taking in information as you read these words. The processes of eating, drinking, or breathing in air are a part of the yin phase. You enter the yin phase when you are drawing in energy, the absorption process. You need energy for the functions of the body and mind; as you take in energy, you also store energy.

YANG EXPANSION

The yang phase is the reutilization of the energy we have taken in. In the yang phase the energy is expanded outward. Turning the pages of this book is a yang process. You are taking the energy you absorbed in the yin phase and using the stored yang energy to turn the page. The yang processes are the actions that involve expanding outward, such as, writing, or peddling a bicycle.

The yin absorption process as well as the yang expansion process is a part of how we breathe energy in and exhale energy out. We will go deeper into this process during our discussion of the Focus Power Breathing Method.

The main goal of this work is not to have you believe in a new system of faith, no matter what your religious affiliation. The goal of this work is to help you experience life as an energetic being, vibrating with Love and Light. When we learn to experience life from the depths of God's radiant power, we begin to experience the intensely spiritual balancing power of God's creation.

When we look at life, our bodies, and the multitude of other physical manifestations we see throughout creation, this is just the beginning – the tip of the iceberg. In other words, there are still many levels of awareness which await our developing consciousness.

For instance, when we look at a car, we may notice the two doors and wheels; behind the car, we may notice the trunk. When standing in front of the car we may notice the front bumper, the hood, the windshield and the steering wheel. While underneath the car, we become aware of the muffler, and brake lines. Every angle offers a different perspective and level of awareness.

However, when your grandmother looks at the car, she may have a lesser degree of awareness, while your mechanic's awareness goes much deeper, with much more detail. We might even say that he has an inner working knowledge over your grandmother through his training, and conscious awareness about cars.

In the same way most of us have only looked at life with their grandmother's glasses. We have only been looking at life externally. As we delve deeper into this work, the goal is simply to help you gain a deeper, more profound perspective and awareness, enabling you to become conscious of the beauty and power that you already possess.

CHAPTER 7

BREATHE IN GOD'S LOVE AND LIGHT AND MANIFEST YOUR DREAMS

BY WALTER BECKLEY

AWARENESS, CONSCIOUSNESS & ENERGY CENTERS

In the previous chapter we discussed the importance of having a deeper working knowledge about life. In this chapter we will cover the various built-in features that you already have available. We will look at the 4 stages of awareness and growth, and how those experiences manifest in your daily life. We will also look at the 7 stages of consciousness and what the attributes of each stage does to develop deeper levels of awareness. In the last part we will look at the various energy centers on the body, the various entry points, organs and glands which hold the incoming energy, as-well-as the sense organs that are related to their positive or negative expression.

4 STAGES OF AWARENESS AND GROWTH

1. The 1st level of understanding teaches us that there is a higher level of functioning available to us. This higher experience is more expansive than our current experience.

2. The 2nd level of understanding is the action level. This is where we start on an actual path of action, seeking to learn about experiencing level one.

BREATHE IN GOD'S LOVE AND LIGHT AND MANIFEST YOUR DREAMS

BY WALTER BECKLEY

3. On the 3rd level we learn to cultivate the qualities and essence of God's Love and Light. From our connection and experience, we transform from our normal everyday experience into a deeper, more meaningful life connection with the Divine.

4. At the 4th level, as you continue the momentum of transforming your life into a spiritual union with the Divine, your mind becomes still. Your body is strengthened, your emotions balanced, and your awareness is clear and keen. This is a silent witnessing state of awareness.

At this level, your consciousness begins to merge into the unconscious realm; the unconscious state begins to melt and integrate with the conscious state. This process continues until the lines that divide consciousness and unconsciousness disappear, and no longer hold the individual captive. At this level, the individual has merged deeper into the Divine realm of experience and is breathing and bathing in God's Oneness. True freedom begins when we disappear and the Divine experience of God appears.

BREATHE IN GOD'S LOVE AND LIGHT AND MANIFEST YOUR DREAMS

BY WALTER BECKLEY

7 STATES OF CONSCIOUSNESS

There are seven states of consciousness, within the human experience. The first three states of consciousness are easily accessible and are the basis of our natural experience in life. The next four states of consciousness are available through the alignment of the mind, body, breath, and emotions with the source of life. The fourth state, the Transcendental state of consciousness, can sometimes be accessed through extraordinary experiences, meditation, prayer, and sometimes through grace. Being in the midst of great danger such as falling off a cliff, spinning during a car accident, or watching a tragic event unfold, sometimes temporarily awakens the fourth state of consciousness, which is a witnessing state of awareness.

The chart below illustrates the levels of unused potential versus divine potential. The Focus Power Personal Development System enhances the divine life potential. By increasing the levels of divine life potential in our waking state, dream state and sleep state of consciousness, we begin to activate the Transcendental state of consciousness. After accessing the Transcendental state, which is the breakthrough point, you begin to ascend into Cosmic consciousness, God consciousness, and Unity states of consciousness.

BREATHE IN GOD'S LOVE AND LIGHT AND MANIFEST YOUR DREAMS

BY WALTER BECKLEY

HIGHER STATES OF CONSCIOUSNESS CHART OF USED AND USED POTENTIAL

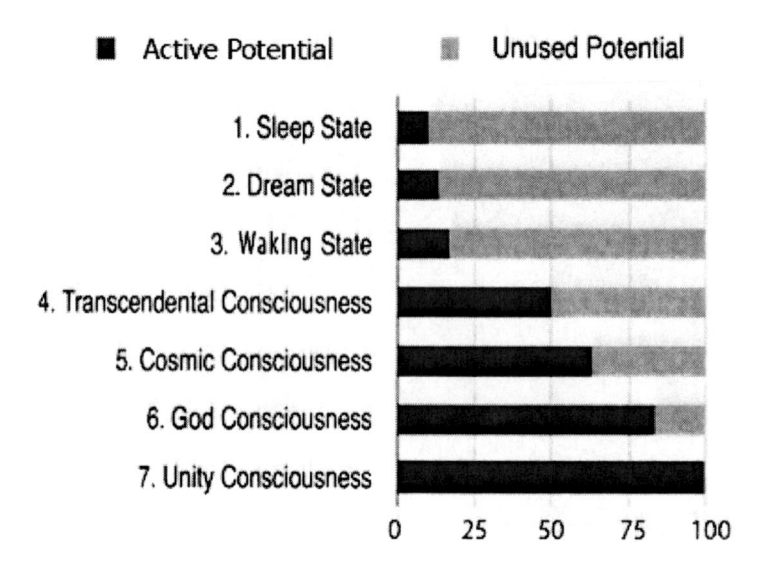

■ Active Potential   ▦ Unused Potential

1. Sleep State	~10
2. Dream State	~12
3. Waking State	~15
4. Transcendental Consciousness	~50
5. Cosmic Consciousness	~65
6. God Consciousness	~80
7. Unity Consciousness	100

Explanation of the 7 states of consciousness:

1. **Sleep state** – dreamless - mind & ego asleep.

2. **Dream state** – REM (Rapid Eye Movement) sleep, mind is active, body is asleep.

3. **Waking state** – daily state of typical 'reality' or wakefulness.

These first three states the mind accesses can be viewed as the first level of a single state of consciousness.

4. **Transcendental consciousness** – a state of restful alertness (silent witness) where the mind is awake but still. This state of consciousness is activated through the Focus Power Personal Development System. This level of consciousness can come up almost anywhere at any given moment of time. As you go in and out of this state of consciousness, your brain wave patterns begin to synchronize. In this state, a person may experience waves of happiness. We momentarily step into this state every time we pass from one state to the other. Each state of consciousness has been defined by scientific research, with definable markings and unique physiology.

5. **Cosmic consciousness** – This state of awareness is often referred to as the first level of awakening or self-realization state of awareness. This is where Transcendental consciousness is a full time experience, underlying the waking, dreaming and sleeping states. The idea of ego is erased and you become the witnessing self, exclusively, for the rest of your life and beyond. You are in a permanent state of enlightened awareness, silently witnessing as the observer of all activity. Fully established in the state of cosmic consciousness, the experience is absolute bliss.

BREATHE IN GOD'S LOVE AND LIGHT AND MANIFEST YOUR DREAMS

BY WALTER BECKLEY

Although the subject (individual) is awake, the object of perception is not yet illuminated. Meaning, objects outside of the individual have not been fully infused with the observer's awareness.

6. **God consciousness** – This state of awareness is also referred to as God realization. After the seeker has spent time in the previous states of consciousness, finer values of perception develop and various centers of energy begin to open. The seeker starts to experience more refined values, full mechanics, and a deeper understanding of the workings of the world, life, and people.

7. **Unity consciousness** – This state of awareness is also referred to as Supreme Oneness, Oneness, or Unity. This state of awareness can be defined by a larger sense of realization - when self is seen in all objects, the realization of "I am that", "thou art that", "all this is that" becomes the individual experience. The duality of subject-object disappears and all illusions end. There is no longer a personal identification; you can still sense yourself as an individual, although you have, for all intents and purposes, become invisible and nonexistent. All distinctions disappear, there is no inside or outside, up or down, good or bad. All pairs of

opposites are experienced as a continuum; it is as if the world out there ceases to exist as being separate. Many paradoxes are resolved through the inclusiveness of oneness.

You have become totally SPIRITUALLY ALIVE!

BREATHE IN GOD'S LOVE AND LIGHT AND MANIFEST YOUR DREAMS

BY WALTER BECKLEY

SPIRITUAL CENTERS

Awareness of the 7 spiritual centers helps enliven and awaken you to the awareness of God's Love and Light, which flows through, connects, and enters into these centers.

ESSENCE OR POWER ACTIVATED	BODY LOCATION
Illumination Center	Soft Spot on top of Head Pineal Gland
Vision Center	Between Eyes Thalamus and hypothalamus Gland
Speech and Dream Center	Throat parathyroid & Thyroid Glands
Love Center	Heart & Thymus Gland
Will Center	Solar Plexus
Creative Center	Prostate & Uterus
Foundation Center	Bottom of Torso

Your body is magnificent. When an ocean liner comes upon an iceberg, the captain realizes that the tip of the iceberg is only the beginning. What you see when you look at your physical body is only the beginning. When the surgeon looks into the body and marvels at all that he sees, he also realizes that he stands on the threshold of

www.GodsLoveandLight.com/higherlearning

BREATHE IN GOD'S LOVE AND LIGHT AND MANIFEST YOUR DREAMS

BY WALTER BECKLEY

just the beginning. When the spiritual initiate sees the source of God's divine Love and Light within himself for the first time, he realizes that he stands on the threshold of the beginning and understanding of just how powerful God is.

By utilizing The Focus Power Personal Development System, you will begin to activate more of God's Love and Light through your body. This conscious connection will help strengthen and heal the body, clear the mind, and balance the emotions.

There are seven major entry points where energy enters the body. The subtle energy that enters into these points gently flows throughout the body's invisible pathways. These invisible pathways are referred to in Chinese medicine as meridians.

The seven major entry and exit points are:

1. Eyes
2, Ears
3. Nose
4. Mouth
5. Skin
6. Anus
7. Sexual Organ

BREATHE IN GOD'S LOVE AND LIGHT AND MANIFEST YOUR DREAMS

BY WALTER BECKLEY

A weakness in the flow of life energy throughout your body's mind and emotional systems could be causing difficulties in the following areas of your life:

- Mental agitations
- Emotional imbalance
- Physical health
- Spiritual disconnection
- Financial lack
- Creative deficiency
- Sexual difficulties

When you learn to activate and replenish your life with God's Love and Light, you will reinvigorate every aspect of your life. God's essence is the force of life which commands your emotions, illuminates the mind, and activates the healing power of love, overcoming all weaknesses in your life. This is nothing new; you were born of the Divine Creator's Love. You have only been out of alignment with his power.

The Focus Power Personal Development System is based on the purest healing power in disciplines which come from the ancient texts and the Holy Bible. This is a natural method, showing how you breathe in God's love in light.

BREATHE IN GOD'S LOVE AND LIGHT AND MANIFEST YOUR DREAMS

BY WALTER BECKLEY

CHALLENGES IN THE FLOW OF LOVE AND LIGHT

Spiritual Center	Challenges	Body Location
Illumination Center	Mental Agitations	Top of Head & Pineal Gland
Vision Center	Emotional Imbalance	Between The Eyes Hypothalamus & Thalamus Gland
Speech and Dream Center	Physical Health	Throat Parathyroid & Thyroid Glands
Love Center	Spiritual Disconnection	Heart & Thymus Gland
Will Center	Financial Lack	Solar Plexus Adrenal Glands
Creative Center	Doom Un-imaginative	Prostate for Men & Uterus/Ovaries for Women
Foundation Base Center	Sexual Difficulties	Perineum Coccyx & Base of Spine

BREATHE IN GOD'S LOVE AND LIGHT AND MANIFEST YOUR DREAMS

BY WALTER BECKLEY

BALANCE IN THE FLOW OF LOVE AND LIGHT

Spiritual Center	Balanced Manifestation	Body Location
Illumination Center	Clarity of Mind	Top of Head & Pineal Gland
Vision Center	Nourishing Relationships	Between the Eyes Hypothalamus & Thalamus Gland
Speech and Dream Center	Commands Speak into Action	Throat & Thyroid Glands
Love Center	Spiritual Unfolding	Heart & Thymus Gland
Will Center	Enrichment Financial	Solar Plexus Adrenal Glands
Creative Center	Creativity and Career Oriented	Prostate for Men & Uterus/Ovaries for Women
Foundation Base Center	Harmony In Life	Perineum Coccyx/Base of Spine

CHAPTER 8

BREATHE IN GOD'S LOVE AND LIGHT AND MANIFEST YOUR DREAMS

BY WALTER BECKLEY

BREATHING IN GOD
BREATHING IN FULFILLMENT

Although the average adult breathes between 18,000 - 30,000 times per day, we usually take breathing for granted. We only become more conscious of our breath during stressful situations. It is when we are sick, worried, or scared that we realize just how important our breath is to our body's support systems. When we are born into this world, the doctor looks for the very first sign of life, which is our breathing.

When we look at the hierarchy of needs, the most vital components needed for sustaining life, we must recognize the breath as being number one. You can survive for 3 to 5 days without water and a month or more without food, but the absence of breath for even a few minutes, can bring about death.

How we breathe is basically the same for each person; you inhale air and you exhale air or carbon dioxide. Some people have shorter inhales and longer exhales, while others have longer inhales and shorter exhales. Or they may have any other combination of longer and shorter breaths.

BREATHE IN GOD'S LOVE AND LIGHT AND MANIFEST YOUR DREAMS

BY WALTER BECKLEY

Have you ever stopped to think about how stress and other daily pressures affect your breathing? If you're like most people, you're being pulled in many different directions throughout your day. Your physical body is under stress, and your mind is constantly occupied with everything that is happening in your life. The negativity from stressful experiences in the body, mind, and emotions, has an effect on how we breathe or barely breathe throughout the entirety of the body.

THE PROPER BREATHING PROCESS

Let's establish a baseline for normal or natural breathing. With natural breathing, a person inhales clean air/oxygen through his nose or mouth into the lungs, filling the lungs with fresh clean air/oxygen. The air is distributed via the lungs into the blood system, enriching the blood cells with oxygen. Simultaneously, there is also an exchange taking place within the cells as the fresh new oxygen is entering and being exchanged for used air and carbon dioxide. Fresh air comes in, carbon dioxide goes out. This is a simplified version; this natural form of breathing is required to maintain good mental and physical health. Taking in nice full breaths of air and releasing old air in a very even and consistent manner is known as proper breathing.

BREATHE IN GOD'S LOVE AND LIGHT AND MANIFEST YOUR DREAMS

BY WALTER BECKLEY

It is well documented that proper breathing, deep breathing, is essential for sustaining life and cleansing our inner body systems. Simply by learning proper breathing techniques, stressful situations and mental agitation decrease while physical health improves. Unfortunately, we usually discover how important a given aspect of our breath is after we start to lose it or have lost it. Proper breathing is vital to the harmony of your emotions, the clarity of your mind, and the overall quality of your life. The negativity from stressful experiences in the body, mind, and emotions has an effect on how we breathe.

DISCONNECTED BREATHING

Most healthy people are born with the ability to breathe into their lungs in a natural and healthy way. However, life can add stress and restrictions to this natural process.

When you are not breathing and connecting with your inner source of power, then you are not allowing your creative potential to be accessed. This situation is called "disconnected breathing." By not consciously breathing in God's Love and Light, you are enabling various forms of toxins, and trauma to formulate within the physical, mental and emotional states of your being. Disconnected breathing creates negative feelings, thoughts, and ideas.

BREATHE IN GOD'S LOVE AND LIGHT AND MANIFEST YOUR DREAMS

BY WALTER BECKLEY

When you consciously learn to breathe in God's Love and Light, you will begin to enjoy vibrant health, more confidence, mental alertness, and a calmness which will bring about a positive attitude and a greater sense of purpose.

At first it may appear somewhat difficult to break your current habit of disconnected breathing and consciously breathe in God's Love and Light. However, as you learn to cultivate your breath, using my breathing system, you will easily become conscious of God's Essence riding within your breath, into every aspect of your life.

WATCHING YOUR BODY BREATHE

Right now I want you to pay attention to the number of times your breathing changes from soft to hard, fast to slow, shallow to deep, and long to short. Notice how often you stop or hold your breath before exhaling. You'll find that you have little or no control over your breathing, especially during various forms of activity, such as bending, lifting, running, and sometimes even just walking.

As you learn to breathe the Focus Power Breathing way, you'll learn to relax and become wakefully alert at the same time. As you learn to watch and take command of your breathing, you'll be amazed at how important your breathing patterns are, in affecting your bodily functions.

THE IMPORTANCE OF THE BREATH

Think about it: If your breath were to stop flowing in and out of your body, first you'd pass out and then you'd die. It would only take a few minutes. On the other hand, with proper breathing you draw more energy into your body and become stronger.

Learn to activate, cultivate and circulate this inner connection. The Focus Power Breathing Method will give you an overall sense of well-being. There is hidden power within your breath. There are thousands upon thousands of writings throughout history attesting to the power of the breath. The Focus Power Breathing Method is designed to help you access and release your inner source of power. Within your body, that inner source of power manifests itself as bioelectrical energy.

The ancient Chinese healing and martial arts systems—including acupuncture, tai chi and qigong (chi kung)—all work by recognizing and cultivating qi, the life force or bioelectrical energy. This energy flows through the body's meridian system. In much the same way that veins carry blood, the meridians carry electrical energy throughout the body. Modern imaging technologies—including electroencephalograms (EEGs), positron emission tomography (PET) and functional magnetic resonance imaging (fMRI)—have been used in the study of qi-based practices, such as acupuncture and meditation.

In China, qigong is an ancient art. Loosely translated, it means "breathing energy exercise." The term "qi" (or chi) refers to the body's vital energy or life force. "Gong" (or "kung") means discipline or exercise. Their combination describes the practice of activating and directing the body's life force, its bioelectrical energy. In particular, qigong refers to a meditative practice that features controlled breathing and slow, graceful movements designed to strengthen an individual's qi.

Masters and serious practitioners of qigong are known for some amazing feats. For example, a student of qigong can achieve what's known as an "Iron Shirt." Individuals who do so, can easily withstand powerful strikes to the body without discomfort. They do so by using their minds, controlled breathing, and coordinated movements that redirect their vital qi to protect various parts of the body.

BREATHE IN GOD'S LOVE AND LIGHT AND MANIFEST YOUR DREAMS

BY WALTER BECKLEY

HOW AND WHY DOES BREATHING THE BREATH OF GOD'S LOVE AND LIGHT MAKE LIFE BETTER?

Infinite power awaits you when you turn inward and connect with your internal stillness. This quality is innate and is the foundation of every human being. Once again this is a gift from the Creator, and it is this divine internal power that sources all of life. This Divine Source animates your body, mind, and emotions. It contributes to the totality of all of your life's known and unknown experiences.

This Divine Source of power is undying; it can never be reborn because it was never born. It has always been and will always be. This Divine Source of power just changes bodies; much like you get into one car, then get out and into another. This power within you has cloaked the self with an individual prospective that you now identify as you, which is your soul. Your cloaked soul is an accumulation of all your life experiences. Combined, they make up the totality of this very moment in time - the expression of you.

The goal of focused breathing is to assist you in gently tearing through the veil of time and illusion. It recharges your conscious awareness with the illumination of God's Love and Light, enabling you to release, forgive and transmute all of the covering which blocks your true relationship with God's healing power.

Think of a car that is driven across many different terrains, in various weather conditions, and whose windshield has picked up dirt, mud, dust, sand, and lots of bugs. With all of that debris, the windshield of the car can become blurred. Let us use this same analogy for our conscious vision and unconscious experience in life. You too may have picked up random materials as you have traveled through life. The effects of stress often distort your ability to understand or see the truth of the present moment. Much like the dirt that can cloud the windshield, stress can impede your ability to envision and create in accordance with God's will.

Your goal, should you choose to accept it, will be to uncover and release all of the blockages that keep you from experiencing God's grace in your life. The best place to begin this journey is with conscious breathing.

BREATHE IN GOD'S LOVE AND LIGHT AND MANIFEST YOUR DREAMS

BY WALTER BECKLEY

CONSCIOUS BREATHING

There is power within your breath, and there is also a source of power within you. The source of power within you also extends throughout the cosmos. When you breathe, your breath rides upon this source of all power. When you breathe, you are connecting with God's life force. You are activating and enhancing the various functions of your body with this essence. When you are conscious of this, magnificence, gratitude, and compassion become your way of life.

MANIFESTING YOUR DREAMS

You are the only one who can watch over the constructs of you mind, body and emotions. There is no one else to cultivate your relationship with the Divine Source of power within you. Only you can go within yourself and bring out the richness of who and what you really are.

It is very important that we ask for what we want in life. It is also important that we place ourselves in the best position to receive that for which we ask, by attending to the care of our mind, body, and emotions.

To manifest your dreams, most people believe that all you have to do is think about them or visualize what you want.

BREATHE IN GOD'S LOVE AND LIGHT AND MANIFEST YOUR DREAMS

BY WALTER BECKLEY

Others believe it's about taking action. Well, they are both right in their own way. First, let's look at the concepts of visualization and action; then we will look at a few other components.

Proverbs 29:18 says, "For lack of vision my people perish." In essence, if you don't have a vision you will surely perish. What is the vision that you hold for your life? When asked that question, people will have a variety of answers: that they don't know; they never thought about it; it wasn't that important; or they will say that God knows their needs. If you have never thought about it, then your vision is to receive exactly what you've been thinking about - which is nothing. Are you getting the idea? What you think about, you bring about.

My point is that you have been employing action and visualization all of your life, knowingly or unknowingly. Have you ever had something that was within your reach but you lost it? Maybe it was a contest, a job, a promotion, or a relationship? Of course you have; we all have! The problem is that you have been operating on the outside of your power or personal essence which is your direct link to the Creator.

BREATHE IN GOD'S LOVE AND LIGHT AND MANIFEST YOUR DREAMS

BY WALTER BECKLEY

There are specific steps you need to take in order to make your vision a reality. These are the steps required to manifest your dream:

1. Strong urge or desire - feeling the need
2. Visualization selection process
3. Ordering process - stating exactly what you want
4. Faith, letting go, knowing that it is on its way
5. Gratitude, receiving what is

Does this process work 100% of the time? Yes, however it depends on the freedom that you are experiencing within. Let me explain. If someone's car has been in a bad accident and the front end is smashed in, would you agree that the car needs some work before you take it on a long trip? Well, the same has happened to 99.99% of the population. Their lives are sputtering along with a multitude of emotional and mental problems. When the mind is overburdened with excessive thoughts and desires, the ability to focus is impaired. Making the simplest things manifest in life becomes extremely difficult. Manifestation is made easy when the mind, body, and emotions are clear and in balance.

BREATHE IN GOD'S LOVE AND LIGHT AND MANIFEST YOUR DREAMS

BY WALTER BECKLEY

The goal of the Focus Power Breathing Method is to start bringing the mind, body, and emotions into a more balanced state and style of functioning. As you move into the advanced levels, it is important that you take your time and practice each stage until you feel a sense of completeness and mastery.

BREATHE IN GOD'S LOVE AND LIGHT AND MANIFEST YOUR DREAMS

BY WALTER BECKLEY

Chapter 9

BREATHE IN GOD'S LOVE AND LIGHT AND MANIFEST YOUR DREAMS

BY WALTER BECKLEY

THE FOCUS POWER PERSONAL DEVELOPMENT SYSTEM

The Focus Power Personal Development System is the most natural way to aid in your expansion and experience in life. It adds a vibrancy of richness, joy and fullness to life, gently penetrating the body in a systematic way, with oxygen and abdominal movements.

Although the system is not a religion, different religious organizations will find it extremely useful in helping to enliven and balance the essential nature of man. It is said that various forms of prayer, breathing, baptizing, and meditation are referred to as "the art of dying." It is a way to release, forgive and transform the old you; the unwanted parts of you. You can then upgrade and be reborn, whole and complete, filled with a more loving and joyful experience of life.

Within the Focus Power Personal Development System we utilize the Focus Power Breathing Method to activate the inner connection of our breath to the Divine Breath of God's Love and Light.

BREATHE IN GOD'S LOVE AND LIGHT AND MANIFEST YOUR DREAMS

BY WALTER BECKLEY

THE FOCUS POWER BREATHING METHOD

Life starts and ends with your breath. The quality of your life is the direct product of how well you breathe. However, in order to breathe correctly and be able to direct your breath throughout your body, it is important to practice and master each lesson without skipping ahead or moving on to the next lesson. As you practice, you will naturally oxygenate your blood cells and your blood vessels. This increased oxygenation helps cleanse toxins from the blood, improving the quality and clarity of the mind.

Through Focus Power Breathing, you will consciously activate - and integrate - your awareness of the inner source of power in your body and life. This inner source of power is like a battery with an endless supply of energy. The benefits of this exercise include:

1. Deep oxygenation of the body as a whole.
2. Healthful massage of the abdominal area, its organs and glands, through the abdominal movements associated with this form of deep breathing.
3. Better distribution of blood and energy throughout the body by the deep, diaphragm-based breathing, which acts like an energy pump.

4. Increased focus as the mind becomes clear and concentrates on the flow of energy through the body.
5. Heightened muscle development and overall strengthening.

Focus Power Breathing is an exercise discipline that can help develop and define your muscles, tendons and ligaments. It also aids in grounding the life energy associated with breathing and overall health.

BREATHE IN GOD'S LOVE AND LIGHT AND MANIFEST YOUR DREAMS

BY WALTER BECKLEY

THE EIGHT PHASES OF YOUR LIFE

The Focus Power Breathing Method affects the following eight phases of your life:

1. Physical health
2. Emotional well-being
3. Mental clarity
4. Sexual balance
5. Harmonious relationships
6. Job/Career
7. Lifestyle
8. Spiritual harmony

Our five-minute Focus Power Breathing Method sessions, enable you to attract positive feelings to your life as you learn to deepen and still your mind. As you gently connect to the power within your breath, you will start to access your inner source of power. As you utilize our system you will learn to cultivate a deeper relationship and understanding of how to gain access to your true essence and power which is within you and within others. Our system allows you a greater connection with the power that is within all of life. When you learn to access your greatest good in life, which is your energetic alignment with your inner source of power, you will begin to enhance all phases of your life.

BREATHE IN GOD'S LOVE AND LIGHT AND MANIFEST YOUR DREAMS

BY WALTER BECKLEY

ACTIVATING THE FOCUS POWER BREATHING METHOD

Activating the power within your breath is the starting point for building the radiance of God's Love and Light in your life. This conscious awareness of the breath enlivens the body, allowing the body and its subtle layers of fascia to release and relax. This release and relaxation allow the body to function in harmony within the ocean of energy that supports the body and all of the infinite aspects of life.

As we breathe in, the body is nourished on the inhale (the Yang phase) and is detoxified on the exhale (the Yin phase). As you inhale, the body is electrically charged with positive Chi energy; and as we exhale, negative Yin energy leaves the body releasing the used Chi energy and air.

When we breathe in through the nose, our sinus and lung cavities fill up by drawing fresh air into the brain and other organs, filling the blood cells with each breath. As the blood cells circulate through the body, the cells which travel closer to the lungs and sinus cavities will receive more chi energy from each breath. The fresh chi travels on the waves of oxygen. The chi enters and follows the breath into the cells, enforcing the electrical current of life which animates the cells, organs, bones, and skin. In essence, the radiant life force nourishes our ability to experience life.

INTERNAL AND EXTERNAL EXERCISES

Your body benefits from both external and internal exercises. Running, weight-lifting, and aerobics are all forms of external exercises; they aid in building the physical attributes of the body. Internal exercises align the subtle energetic life force which flows through the invisible pathways inside the body. They cultivate and regulate the flow of this Divine Power until peak release is established and the body lets go completely; the Divine takes over, unregulated. When you breathe through the Focus Power Breathing Method, you will strengthen the flow of God's Love and Light.

BREATHE IN GOD'S LOVE AND LIGHT AND MANIFEST YOUR DREAMS

BY WALTER BECKLEY

INTERNAL EXERCISES

There are internal exercises which can:

- Activate and open your inner pathways.
- Help you gather and store energy inside your body.
- Assist you in expanding your energy in life.

These internal exercises create a gentle cushion, much like hydraulic shocks on a car. They allow the divine oil of Love and Light to build up in the body, creating an internal cushion which protects you from the bumps and bruises that life may throw at you.

When the power of God's Love and Light is activated in your body, you feel protected and strengthened in a subtle, clean, and dynamic way. You will also feel a dramatically different style of thinking which we refer to as clear mind, empty or no mind, or my favorite: a beautiful mind.

At first, connecting with this part of the training program may seem difficult. But when you learn to activate the power within your body using this method, you will understand the beauty and power of this all-important connection. You'll gain the ability to calm your body, mind, and emotions.

At its highest level, the method becomes blissful breathing. It is important to understand that there is unlimited power in the air that moves in and out of your body, and you are about to learn how to connect with that power.

BREATHE IN GOD'S LOVE AND LIGHT AND MANIFEST YOUR DREAMS

BY WALTER BECKLEY

ACTIVATING THE POWER WITHIN THE BREATH

Find a comfortable chair, one that has a stationary back. Do not use a swivel chair or a chair with rollers. Sit towards the front half of your chair, straight up without using the back rest. Rest your palms face up on your thighs, with relaxed open hands. Your head should be even and the bottom of your chin tucked in slightly.

All breathing will take place through your nose, unless your nasal passages are stuffy. Breathing through the nose will help you develop a deeper level of command over your breath. It also helps filter dust, dirt, and airborne pathogens. When you breathe only through your mouth, you give an open invitation for germs to enter into your body.

As you go deeper into breathing in through your nose, you will cleanse and heal the sinus cavity, allowing more oxygen to flow into the brain. This extra oxygen invigorates the blood by cleansing toxins more rapidly. It also helps clear the mind and improve the creativity and power of your mind. A big part of what we will be practicing and working to cultivate is our awareness of God's Love and Light, which is within you.

BREATHE IN GOD'S LOVE AND LIGHT AND MANIFEST YOUR DREAMS

BY WALTER BECKLEY

THE LOCATION OF YOUR SOURCE CENTER

Many ancient texts discuss the body's original creative center or source center, and the consensus seems to be that it is located just below the navel in the center of the body. This will become apparent as you learn to connect your breath within your body, just below your navel. The actual location of this source center does vary from person to person, depending upon the size of the belly and the distance between the naval and pelvic bone.

The following information should be taken as approximations:

1. If you are thin to medium build, but toned or in great shape –your source center is located approximately two fingers' thickness below your navel.

2. If you are medium build but not toned, or if your belly protrudes, you can locate your source center approximately two or three fingers' thickness below your navel.

3. If you are a much larger person and your belly is large, you may use the halfway point. The halfway point is the distance between the navel and the pelvic bone.

BREATHE IN GOD'S LOVE AND LIGHT AND MANIFEST YOUR DREAMS

BY WALTER BECKLEY

Once you learn to breathe below the navel into your source center, your original source center will start to activate on its own. Many people feel this activation as warmth, tingling, electrical, or flowing like ocean waves inside their body.

BREATHE IN GOD'S LOVE AND LIGHT AND MANIFEST YOUR DREAMS

BY WALTER BECKLEY

FOCUS POWER BREATHING METHOD
ACTIVATION PROCESS LEVEL 1

Inhale

1. Be aware of your breath as you inhale.
2. Be aware of your breath expanding your abdomen area like a balloon being filled with air.
3. Feel very comfortable and easy as you inhale focusing below your navel.
4. Feel your Source Center, a space inside the center of your body below the navel.

(See illustration on page 153)

Exhale

1. Be aware of your breath as you exhale.
2. Be aware of your breath leaving your abdomen area as you flatten your stomach towards your back.
3. Feel very comfortable and easy as you exhale focusing below your navel.
4. Feel your Source Center, a space inside the center of your body below the navel

(See illustration on page 154)

| BREATHE IN GOD'S LOVE AND LIGHT AND MANIFEST YOUR DREAMS | BY WALTER BECKLEY |

INHALE

Inhale

Navel Area Expands Out

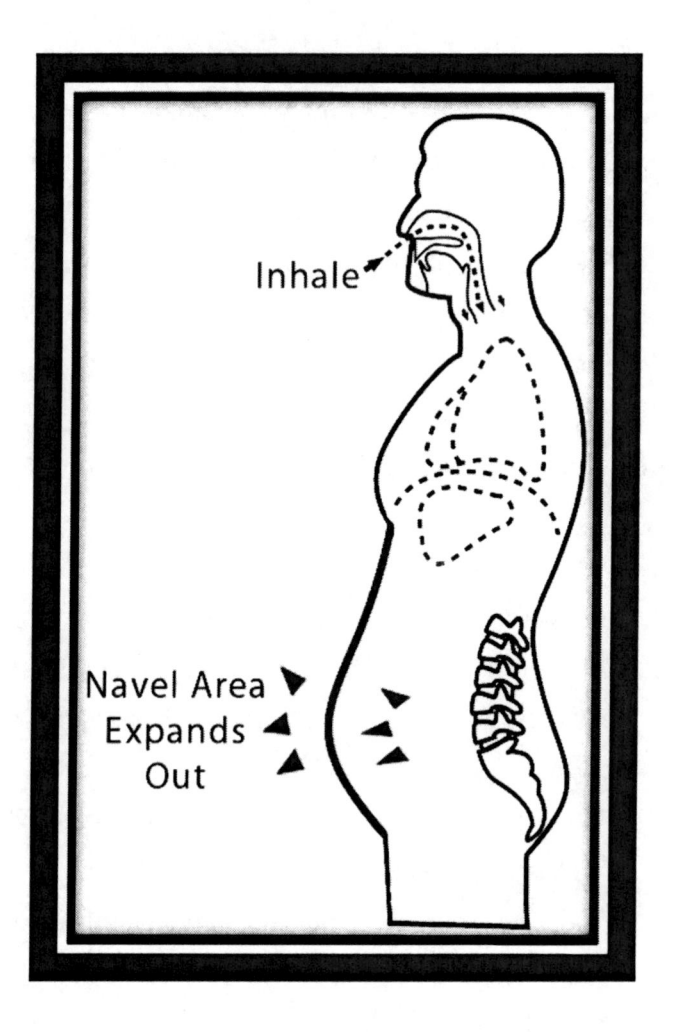

As you inhale, feel the breath filling the body as your navel area expands out.

www.GodsLoveandLight.com/higherlearning Page 154

BREATHE IN GOD'S LOVE AND LIGHT AND MANIFEST YOUR DREAMS

BY WALTER BECKLEY

EXHALE

Exhale

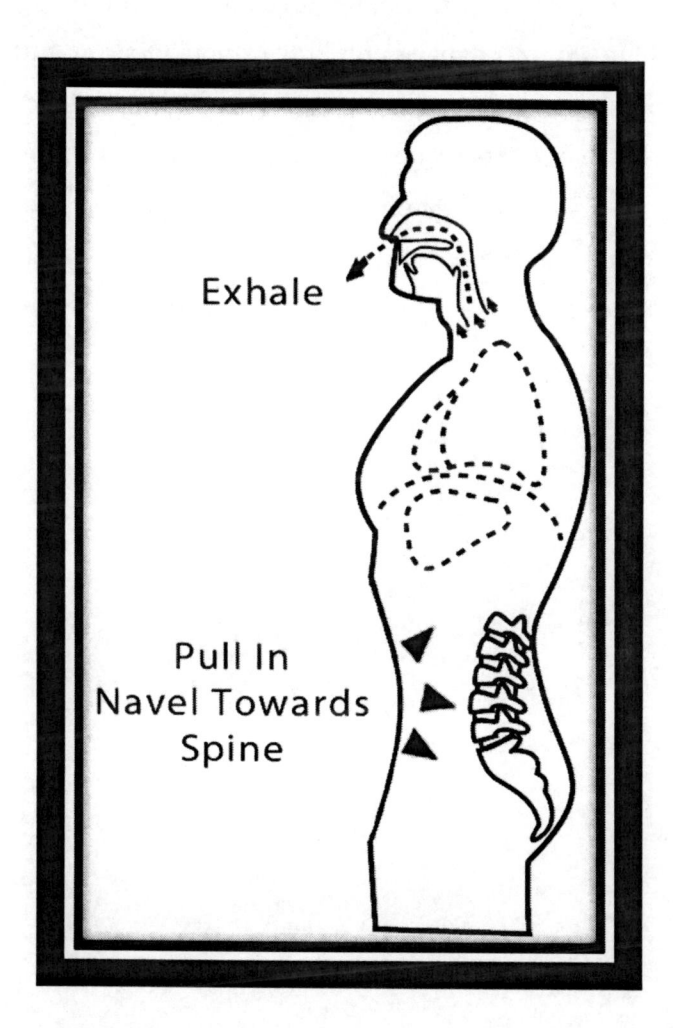

Pull In Navel Towards Spine

As you exhale, feel the breath leaving the body as your navel area flattens in towards the spine.

BREATHE IN GOD'S LOVE AND LIGHT AND MANIFEST YOUR DREAMS

BY WALTER BECKLEY

BASIC INSTRUCTIONS

When you inhale or exhale, breathe only through the nose. Your mouth should be relaxed with teeth slightly touching, not too tight or grinding. As you inhale do not try to follow your breath down into your body. Instead, be aware of your breath instantly connecting with the navel area as it expands. When you exhale, keep your mind at the navel as the breath leaves your abdominal area. Continue to nurture your breath in this manner.

BREATHE IN GOD'S LOVE AND LIGHT AND MANIFEST YOUR DREAMS

BY WALTER BECKLEY

OCEAN BREATHING MUSIC

The various levels of Focus Power Breathing involve using a musical CD entitled Ocean Breathing. The rhythm and pulse of ocean breathing enables you to connect with and start to feel the rhythm of your breath and energy. The music is like the inner movement of your inner sound. Your body has a sound it makes much like each factory makes its own unique sound. When your breath and inner source of power become united, the inner fire ignites. Inside the fire, you will sense a vibration that feels like joy. Some people also report a warm or tingling quality. Find this inner joy, and lose yourself in it.

This ocean breathing music came through me as I endeavored to awaken the healing power within. I offer this musical cadence in order to help promote inner growth, balance, healing power and radiance.

BREATHE IN GOD'S LOVE AND LIGHT AND MANIFEST YOUR DREAMS

BY WALTER BECKLEY

LESSON 1 – FOCUS POWER BREATHING METHOD INSTRUCTIONS

The first technique you will learn is entitled "The Activation Breath." This method will begin your activation process of God's Love and Light. You can begin by listening to the first track of the Ocean Breathing CD or you can simply count along until you have access to the Ocean Breathing music.

1. Sit up straight.
2. Place your feet flat against the floor.
3. Set your hands over your navel, or rest them on your thighs with palms facing up.
4. Inhale (for a count of 4 or 5 seconds)—as you count and inhale, your navel area should expand.
5. Exhale (for a count of 4 or 5 seconds)—and as you count and exhale, your navel area should contract in towards your spine.
6. Breathe only through your nose.
7. Close your eyes.
8. Be very gentle.
9. Repeat this sequence for about five minutes.

Practice Focus Power Breathing twice a day: First thing in the morning and an hour before or after dinner. The counting method will help you understand the movement and flow of the breath. However, the Ocean Breathing CD will allow you to continuously focus on just your breath, rather than keeping your mind busy with counting.

RESTING PHASE

The last part of your internal cultivation and fitness program is to just rest. Just lie on your back and rest. You can also sit back comfortably in a reclining chair and rest with your hands at your sides or in your lap. Give yourself permission to do nothing - just disappear into emptiness, stillness, and silence.

When you have a basic understanding and deeper connection with this first level of Focus Power Breathing- the 5-minute session, proceed to the next track for the 20-minute session. Remember, for maximum benefit, sit up with your feet flat against the floor, hands relaxed, resting on your legs.

BREATHE IN GOD'S LOVE AND LIGHT AND MANIFEST YOUR DREAMS

BY WALTER BECKLEY

JOURNAL TODAY

Start a diary or journal today. It only takes 5 to 10 minutes to change the disarray of your life into something that aligns with God's blue print. The simplest way to begin your journal would be to look at the 9 phases of your life:

1. Are you physically fit? On a scale from 1 to 10, what level of fitness would you give yourself?
2. Are you emotionally balanced? Do you feel anger, fear, or frustration? What level of emotional stability would you assign to your life?
3. Does your mind feel fresh and clear or are you experiencing confusion, problems getting started, or problems getting things done? What level of mental power would you assign your life?
4. What level from 1 to 10 would you assign to the depth and quality of the relationships in your life?
5. Are you experiencing active and non-active sexual harmony and balance? What level would you assign your sexual creative energies?
6. Are you experiencing the quality of life or lifestyle that you envision for yourself? On a level from 1 to 10, how close are you to receiving exactly what you want in your day-to-day life?

7. Are you doing what you want in life regarding your career? What level would you assign to your current career choice?

8. Are you experiencing the spiritual evolution and growth in life that you desire?

If you find that your levels are all 8s, 9s, and 10s, I would suggest that you change them to 1s, 2s, and 3s in order to enable you to go deeper in evaluating your strengths and weaknesses. Be gentle with yourself, be joyful with this work, and marvel at life!

Your experiences are important, if you have any questions or comments please feel free to send your experience to journal@GodsLoveandLight.com. All testimonies are welcome and will be made available to assist others in their growth.

BREATHE IN GOD'S LOVE AND LIGHT AND MANIFEST YOUR DREAMS

BY WALTER BECKLEY

FOCUS POWER BREATHING
BALANCING THE INHALE AND EXHALE
Advanced Level 1

BALANCING THE INHALE AND EXHALE

The method you are about to learn is entitled "Balancing the Inhale and Exhale." Do not start this method until you have thoroughly practiced the first level, "The Activation Breath" for 20 minutes, twice a day for at least 30 days.

In this lesson you will be building upon what you have already learned in the first lesson "The Activation Breath".

Before you began this program, you inhaled and exhaled without focus. You had no interest in the level of power and volume that you were using during your inhalations and exhalations. Your goal now is to feel the same drawing power being exerted upon your inhale and your exhale equally. In this advance level you will utilize a greater level of awareness and give attention to the quality and volume of how you inhale and exhale into your source center.

BREATHE IN GOD'S LOVE AND LIGHT AND MANIFEST YOUR DREAMS

BY WALTER BECKLEY

BALANCING THE INHALE AND EXHALE INSTRUCTIONS

1. Practice making your inhale and exhale begin and end with the same level of volume, power easiness/gentleness.
2. Your intent is always to feel and connect with God's Love and Light.
3. Inhale a steady stream of air mixed with your intentions on God's Love and Light
4. Exhale the same volume of air mixed with your intentions on God's Love and Light
5. Continue breathing with the Ocean Breathing music for 20 minutes twice a day.
6. Remember to always lie down to rest for 10 to 15 minutes after each session.

BREATHE IN GOD'S LOVE AND LIGHT AND MANIFEST YOUR DREAMS

BY WALTER BECKLEY

FOCUS POWER BREATHING
DEEP ACTIVATION METHOD
Advanced Level 2

The "Deep Activation Method" will enable you to learn to inhale in and exhale out God's Love and Light from the six directions that energy flows into and out of the body and into and out of the source center.

The six directions are the front, back, left and right sides, the head and bottom of the torso or perineum. As you cultivate God's Love and Light you begin to increase the love, joy, light and clarity and decrease the negativity and pain in your life. You will learn a series of 8 variations or forms of breathing which concludes with the Diamond Mind, Golden Body Awareness. This is where the body is clean and clear, and the mind is still and free, and God's Love and Light flows through you reigning supremely over your life.

It is important to build a strong foundation and to do this you will need to spend a minimum of 20 minutes twice a day for 14 days straight cultivating each lesson. If, you miss a day, start over. Some people will need to spend more time on a given lesson; spending more time on any lesson will only make your experience better.

BREATHE IN GOD'S LOVE AND LIGHT AND MANIFEST YOUR DREAMS

BY WALTER BECKLEY

DEEP ACTIVATION METHOD

Do not start this method until you have practiced level 2, "Balancing the Inhale and Exhale" for at 20 minutes twice a day for 30 days.

You are now ready to start developing and using your mind to direct the flow of Love and Light in and out of your body. Through the "Deep Activation Method" of gentle repetition of following the flow of your breath in conjunction with God's Love and Light in and out of your source center while utilizing the various funnels.

Funnels are entry and exit points on the body upon which you will direct the flow of God's Love and Light to and from the body. There are six funnels located on the body or entry and exit points which we will work with over the next 16 weeks. You will spend approximately 14 days on each part. You will start with and work your way into establishing a connection with the following funnels in this order.

1. Front Funnel 2. Back Funnel 3. Combining Front and Back Funnels 4. Right & Left Side Funnels 5. Four Direction (head, back, left and right sides) 6. Head Funnel 7. Bottom Funnel 8. Combining Head and Bottom Funnel 9. Six Direction Combination

BREATHE IN GOD'S LOVE AND LIGHT AND MANIFEST YOUR DREAMS

BY WALTER BECKLEY

Activate all funnels (Front, Back, Right & Left Sides, Head, and Bottom Funnel) on the inhale and exhale at the same time. Follow the directions for each part completely:

| BREATHE IN GOD'S LOVE AND LIGHT AND MANIFEST YOUR DREAMS | BY WALTER BECKLEY |

DEEP

ACTIVATION

BREATHING IN GOD'S LOVE AND LIGHT

YOUR BODY

FUNNELS

BREATHE IN GOD'S LOVE AND LIGHT AND MANIFEST YOUR DREAMS

BY WALTER BECKLEY

REVIEW AND MEMORIZE FONT BODY FUNNEL NAMES AND LOCATIONS

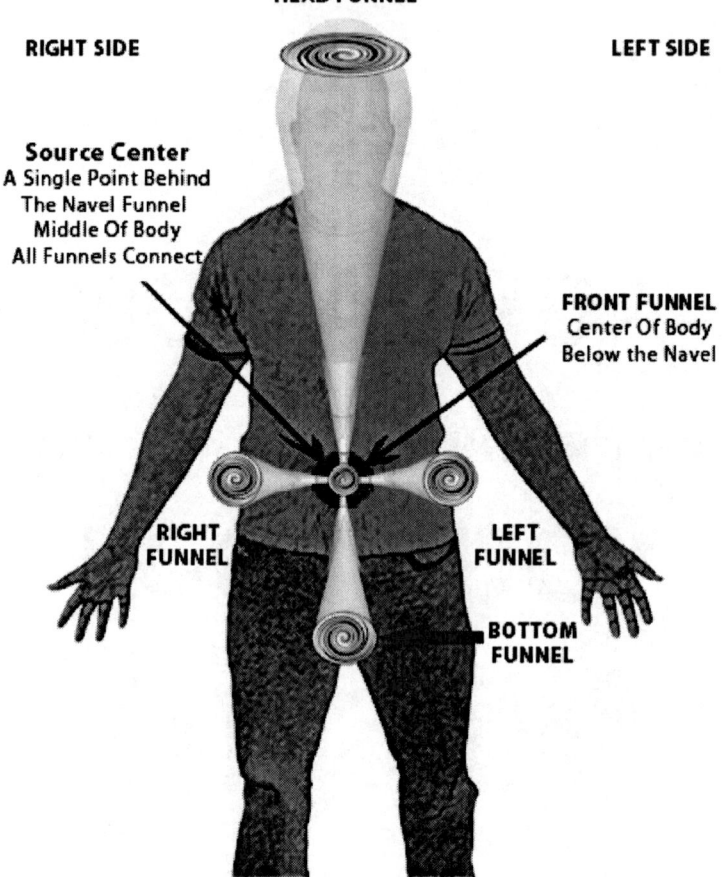

BODY ENERGY FUNNELS

HEAD FUNNEL

RIGHT SIDE

LEFT SIDE

Source Center
A Single Point Behind
The Navel Funnel
Middle Of Body
All Funnels Connect

FRONT FUNNEL
Center Of Body
Below the Navel

RIGHT FUNNEL

LEFT FUNNEL

BOTTOM FUNNEL

www.GodsLoveandLight.com/higherlearning

BREATHE IN GOD'S LOVE AND LIGHT AND MANIFEST YOUR DREAMS

BY WALTER BECKLEY

REVIEW AND MEMORIZE BACK BODY FUNNEL NAMES AND LOCATIONS

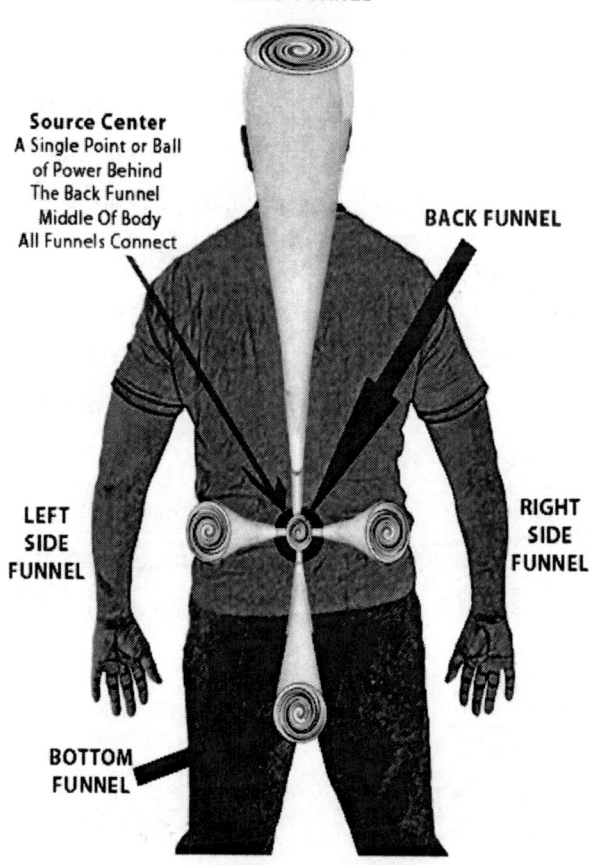

BACK FUNNEL VIEW
HEAD FUNNEL

Source Center
A Single Point or Ball of Power Behind The Back Funnel Middle Of Body All Funnels Connect

BACK FUNNEL

LEFT SIDE FUNNEL

RIGHT SIDE FUNNEL

BOTTOM FUNNEL

www.GodsLoveandLight.com/higherlearning   Page 169

BREATHE IN GOD'S LOVE AND LIGHT AND MANIFEST YOUR DREAMS

BY WALTER BECKLEY

PART 1 - FUNNELING IN 1 DIRECTION - FRONT
INHALE & EXHALE GOD'S LOVE AND LIGHT THROUGH THE FRONT FUNNEL

1. Inhale, funneling God's Love and Light into the source center (see round ball in center of body in illustration (A.1) on the next page), feel the Love and Light; draw the energy straight in or spiral into the source center (See illustration (A.2) on next page).
2. Exhale, funneling and spiraling God's Love and Light out from the source center out the front funnel.
3. Inhale and Exhale, funneling and spiraling God's Love and Light out from the source center.
4. Practice this for 20 minutes twice a day for 14 days.

BREATHE IN GOD'S LOVE AND LIGHT AND MANIFEST YOUR DREAMS

BY WALTER BECKLEY

INHALE & EXHALE OUT THE FRONT FUNNEL

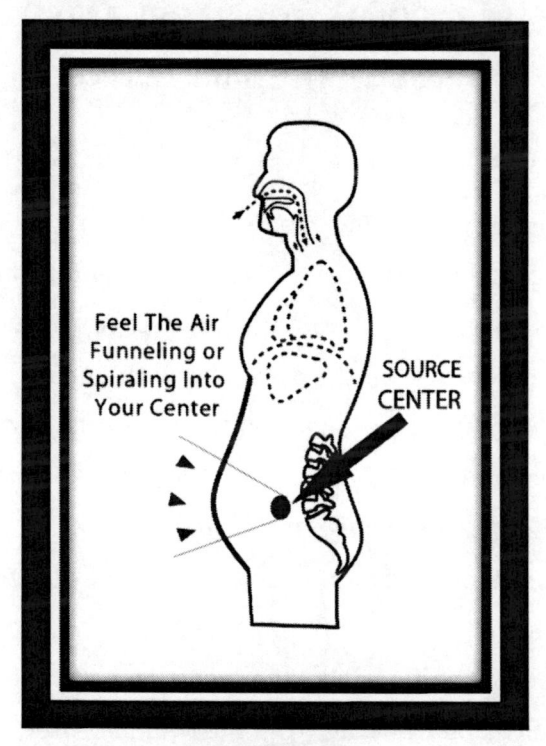

Illustration (A.1)

You may feel your energy moving in a straight line or circling or spiraling into the front funnel into your source center.

Spiraling Energy

Illustration (A.2)

BREATHE IN GOD'S LOVE AND LIGHT AND MANIFEST YOUR DREAMS

BY WALTER BECKLEY

PART 2 - FUNNELING IN 1 DIRECTION - BACK
INHALE & EXHALE GOD'S LOVE AND LIGHT THROUGH THE BACK FUNNEL

1. Inhale, funneling God's Love and Light into the source center (see round ball in center of body in illustration (B.1) on the next page), through the back funnel on the spine; draw the energy straight in or spiral the energy into the source center (See illustration (B.2) on the next page).
2. Exhale, funneling and spiraling God's Love and Light out from the source center out the back funnel.
3. Inhale and Exhale, funneling and spiraling God's Love and Light out from the source center.
4. Practice this for 20 minutes twice a day for 14 days for.

BREATHE IN GOD'S LOVE AND LIGHT AND MANIFEST YOUR DREAMS

BY WALTER BECKLEY

INHALE & EXHALE OUT THE BACK FUNNEL

Feel The Air Funneling or Spiraling Into Your Center

SOURCE CENTER

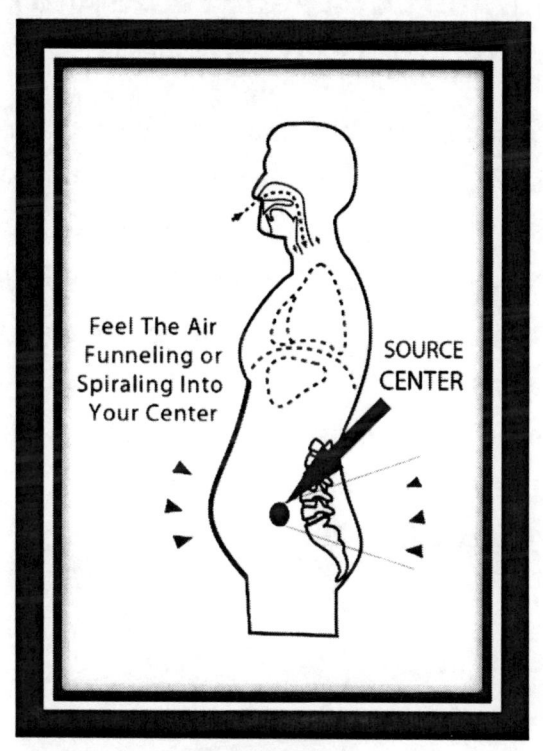

Illustration (B.1)

You may feel your energy moving in a straight line or circling or spiraling into the front funnel into your source center.

Spiraling Energy

Illustration (B.2)

PART 3 – TWO DIRECTION COMBINATION– INHALE AND EXHALE GOD'S LOVE AND LIGHT THROUGH THE FRONT AND BACK FUNNELS

1. Inhale, God's Love and Light from the front and back funnels simultaneously into the source center. (See illustration (B.3) on the next page).
2. Exhale, funneling and spiraling God's Love and Light out from the source center out the back funnel.
3. Inhale and Exhale, funneling and spiraling God's Love and Light out from the source center.
4. Practice this for 20 minutes twice a day for 14 days.

BREATHE IN GOD'S LOVE AND LIGHT AND MANIFEST YOUR DREAMS

BY WALTER BECKLEY

TWO DIRECTION COMBINATION

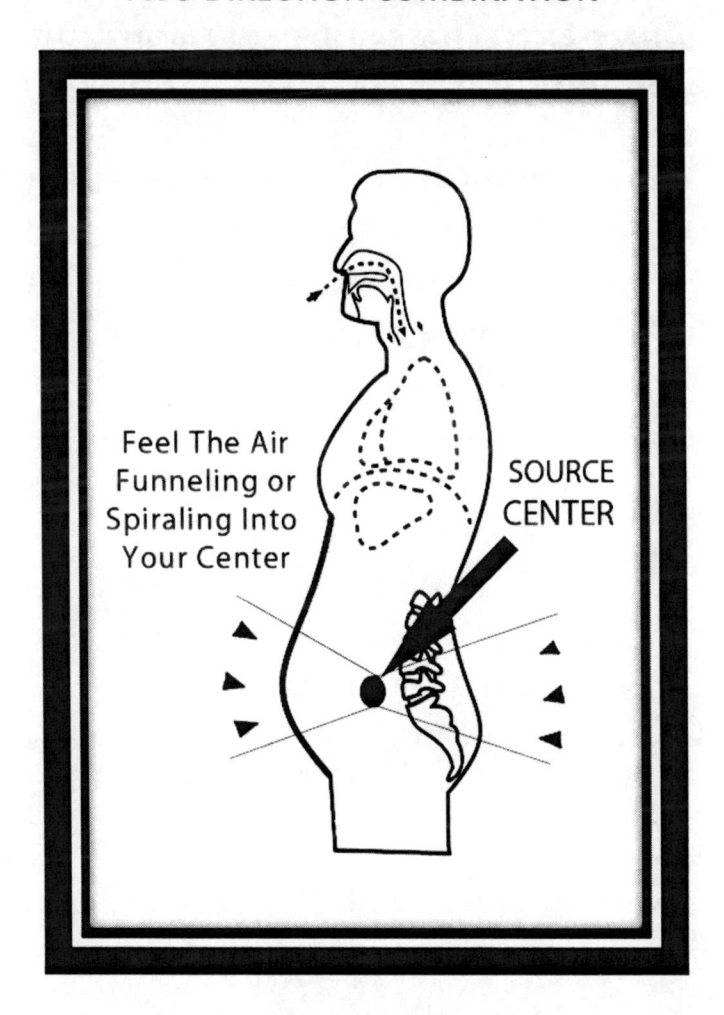

Illustration (B.3)

BREATHE IN GOD'S LOVE AND LIGHT AND MANIFEST YOUR DREAMS

BY WALTER BECKLEY

PART 4 - FUNNELING IN 2 SIDE DIRECTION INHALE AND EXHALE GOD'S LOVE AND LIGHT THROUGH THE LEFT AND RIGHT SIDE FUNNELS

1. Inhale, funneling God's Love and Light into the source center through the left and right side funnels; draw the energy straight in or spiral the energy into the source center (See illustration (C.1) on the next page).
2. Exhale, funneling and spiraling God's Love and Light out from the source center out the left and right side funnels.
3. Inhale and Exhale, funneling and spiraling God's Love and Light in and out from the source center in and out the left and right side funnels.
4. Practice this for 20 minutes twice a day for 14 days for.

BREATHE IN GOD'S LOVE AND LIGHT AND MANIFEST YOUR DREAMS

BY WALTER BECKLEY

LEFT & RIGHT SIDE FUNNELS

SIDE FUNNEL VIEW

Breath Love and Light, In and Out of Your Left and Right Side Funnels... Spiral Into Your Source Center

SOURCE CENTER is Behind Spiraling Funnel Energy

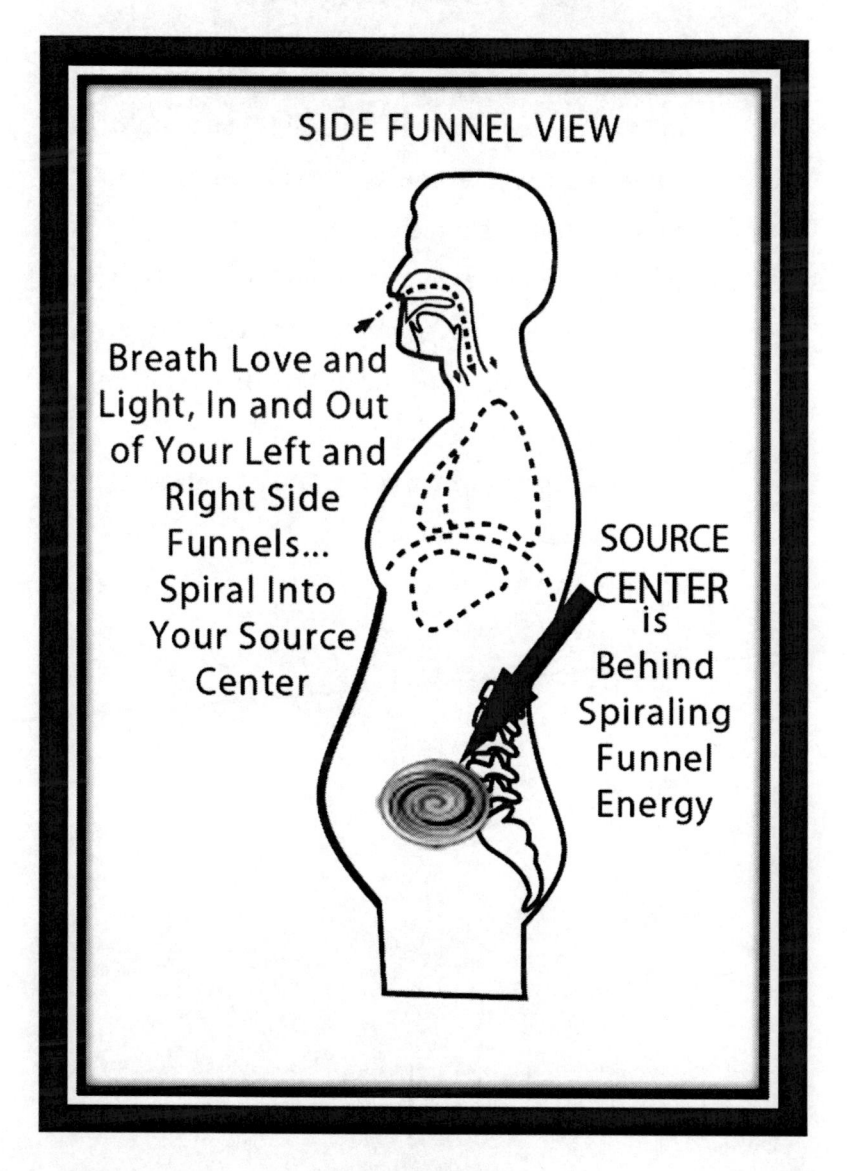

Illustration (C.1)

www.GodsLoveandLight.com/higherlearning   Page 177

BREATHE IN GOD'S LOVE AND LIGHT AND MANIFEST YOUR DREAMS

BY WALTER BECKLEY

PART 5 - FUNNELING IN 4 DIRECTIONS
COMBINE THE FRONT, BACK,
LEFT AND RIGHT SIDES

1. Inhale, funneling God's Love and Light into the source center through the left and right side funnels; draw the energy straight in or spiral the energy into the source center.

2. Exhale, funneling and spiraling God's Love and Light out from the source center out the left and right side funnels (See illustration on next page).

3. Inhale and Exhale, funneling and spiraling God's Love and Light out from the source center out the left and right side funnels.

4. Practice this for 14 days for 20 minutes twice a day.

BREATHE IN GOD'S LOVE AND LIGHT AND MANIFEST YOUR DREAMS

BY WALTER BECKLEY

TOP VIEW - LOOKING DOWN INTO THE BODY BELOW THE NAVEL LEVEL

Inhale and Exhale God's Love and Light
Into Your Source Center

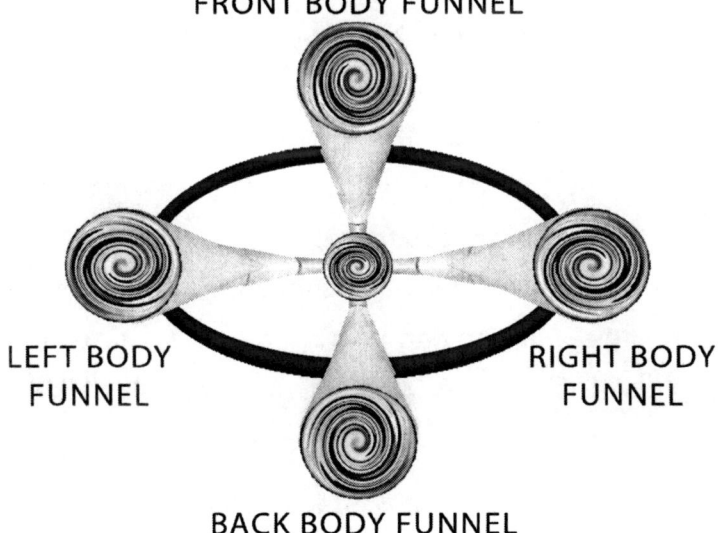

FRONT BODY FUNNEL

LEFT BODY FUNNEL

RIGHT BODY FUNNEL

BACK BODY FUNNEL

BREATHE IN GOD'S LOVE AND LIGHT AND MANIFEST YOUR DREAMS

BY WALTER BECKLEY

PART 6 - INHALE AND EXHALE GOD'S LOVE AND LIGHT THROUGH THE HEAD FUNNEL

1. Inhale, funneling God's Love and Light into the source center through the top of the head funnel; draw the energy straight in or spiral the energy into the source center.
2. Exhale, funneling and spiraling God's Love and Light out from the source center out the head funnel.
3. Inhale and Exhale, funneling and spiraling God's Love and Light in and out from the source center in and out the head funnel.
4. Practice this for 14 days for 20 minutes twice a day. (See illustration (D.1) on the next page).

BREATHE IN GOD'S LOVE AND LIGHT AND MANIFEST YOUR DREAMS

BY WALTER BECKLEY

BODY ENERGY FUNNELS

HEAD FUNNEL

RIGHT SIDE

LEFT SIDE

Source Center
A Single Point Behind
The Navel Funnel
Middle Of Body
All Funnels Connect

FRONT FUNNEL
Center Of Body
Below the Navel

BOTTOM FUNNEL

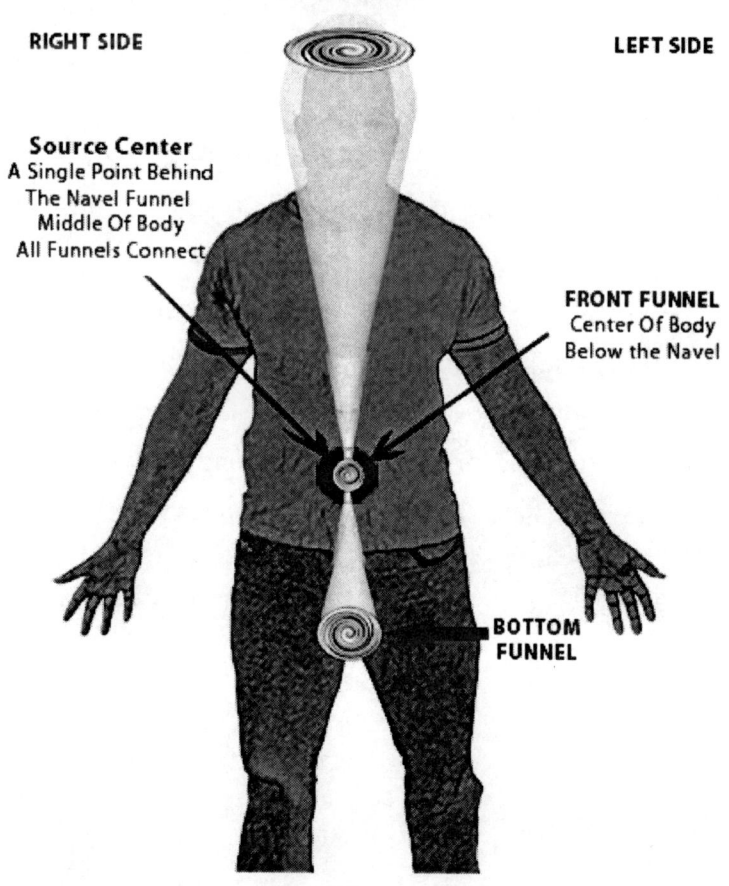

Illustration (D.1)

PART 7- INHALE AND EXHALE GOD'S LOVE AND LIGHT THROUGH THE BOTTOM FUNNEL

1. Inhale, funneling God's Love and Light into the source center through the perineum or bottom funnel; draw the energy straight in or spiral the energy into the source center.
2. Exhale, funneling and spiraling God's Love and Light out from the source center out the bottom funnel.
3. Inhale and Exhale, funneling and spiraling God's Love and Light in and out from the source center in and out the bottom funnel.
4. Practice this for 14 days for 20 minutes twice a day.

(See illustration (D.1) on the previous page)

BREATHE IN GOD'S LOVE AND LIGHT AND MANIFEST YOUR DREAMS

BY WALTER BECKLEY

PART 8 - INHALE AND EXHALE GOD'S LOVE AND LIGHT, THROUGH THE HEAD AND BOTTOM FUNNELS

1. Inhale, funneling God's Love and Light into the source center through the Head and bottom funnels; Inhale from the top of the head down, and from the bottom of the torso perineum up; draw the energy straight in or spiral the energy into the source center..
2. Exhale, funneling and spiraling God's Love and Light out from the source center out the Head and bottom funnels.
3. Inhale and Exhale, funneling and spiraling God's Love and Light in and out from the source center in and out the Head and bottom funnels.
4. Practice this for 14 days for 20 minutes twice a day.

(See illustration (D.1))

BREATHE IN GOD'S LOVE AND LIGHT AND MANIFEST YOUR DREAMS

BY WALTER BECKLEY

PART 9 - INHALE AND EXHALE GOD'S LOVE AND LIGHT, THROUGH THE SIX DIRECTIONS

1. Inhale, funneling God's Love and Light into the source center through the front, back, left side, right side, head and bottom funnels; draw the energy straight in or spiral the energy into the source center..
2. Exhale, funneling and spiraling God's Love and Light out from the source center out the front, back, left side, right side, head and bottom funnels.
3. Inhale and Exhale, funneling and spiraling God's Love and Light in and out from the source center in and out the front, back, left side, right side, head and bottom funnels.
4. This will become your daily cultivation sessions thus assisting you embodying the Diamond Mind, Golden Body Awareness

(See illustrations (E.1, E.2, E3) on the next page)

BREATHE IN GOD'S LOVE AND LIGHT AND MANIFEST YOUR DREAMS

BY WALTER BECKLEY

FUNNELING IN 6 DIRECTIONS - TOP OF HEAD AND BOTTOM OF TORSO

BODY ENERGY FUNNELS

HEAD FUNNEL

RIGHT SIDE

LEFT SIDE

Source Center
A Single Point Behind
The Navel Funnel
Middle Of Body
All Funnels Connect

NAVEL FUNNEL
Center Of Body
Below the Navel

RIGHT FUNNEL

LEFT FUNNEL

BOTTOM FUNNEL

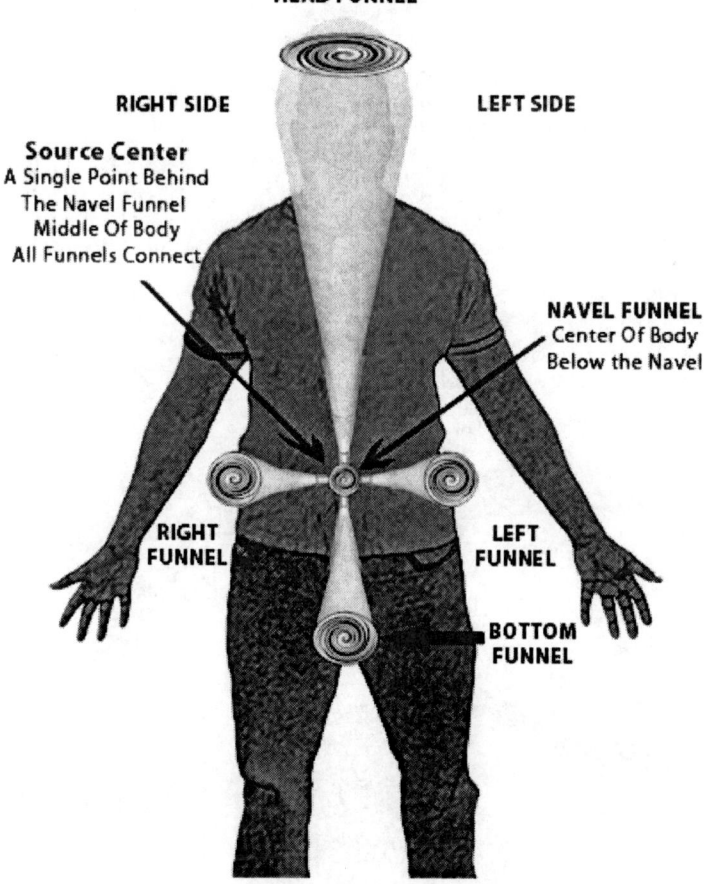

Illustration (E1,)

www.GodsLoveandLight.com/higherlearning

BREATHE IN GOD'S LOVE AND LIGHT AND MANIFEST YOUR DREAMS

BY WALTER BECKLEY

SIDE FUNNEL VIEW

HEAD FUNNEL

Source Center
A Single Point Behind The Side Funnel And Inbetween The Front And Back Funnel
- All Funnels Connect

SIDE FUNNEL

BOTTOM FUNNEL

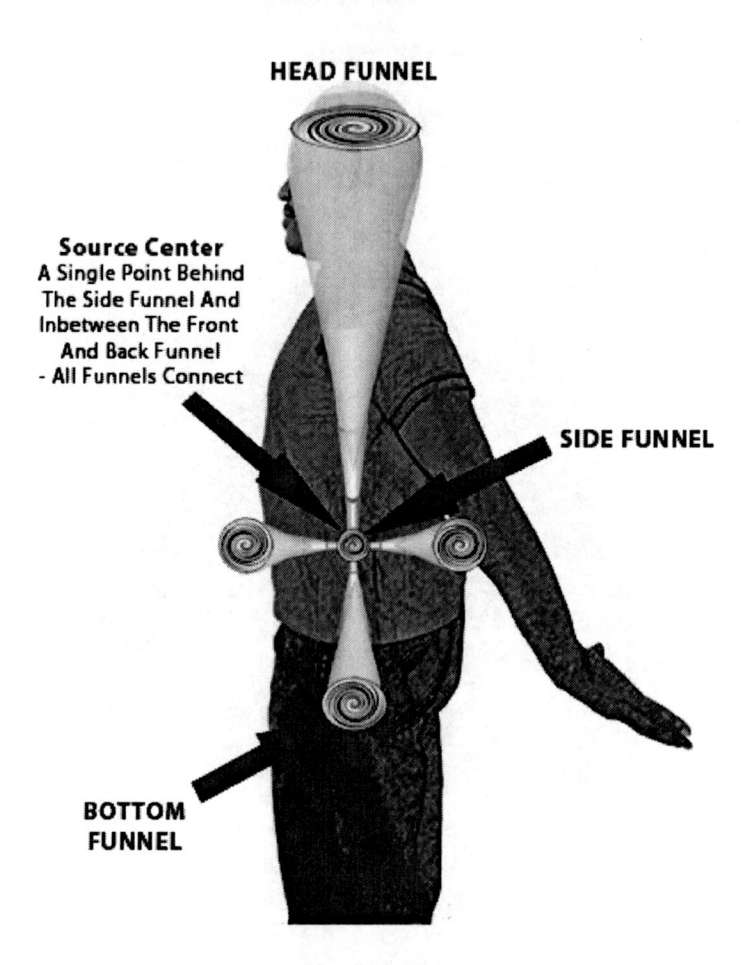

Illustration (E.2)

| BREATHE IN GOD'S LOVE AND LIGHT AND MANIFEST YOUR DREAMS | BY WALTER BECKLEY |

BACK FUNNEL VIEW

HEAD FUNNEL

Source Center
A Single Point Behind
The Navel Funnel
Middle Of Body
All Funnels Connect

BACK FUNNEL

LEFT SIDE FUNNEL

RIGHT SIDE FUNNEL

BOTTOM FUNNEL

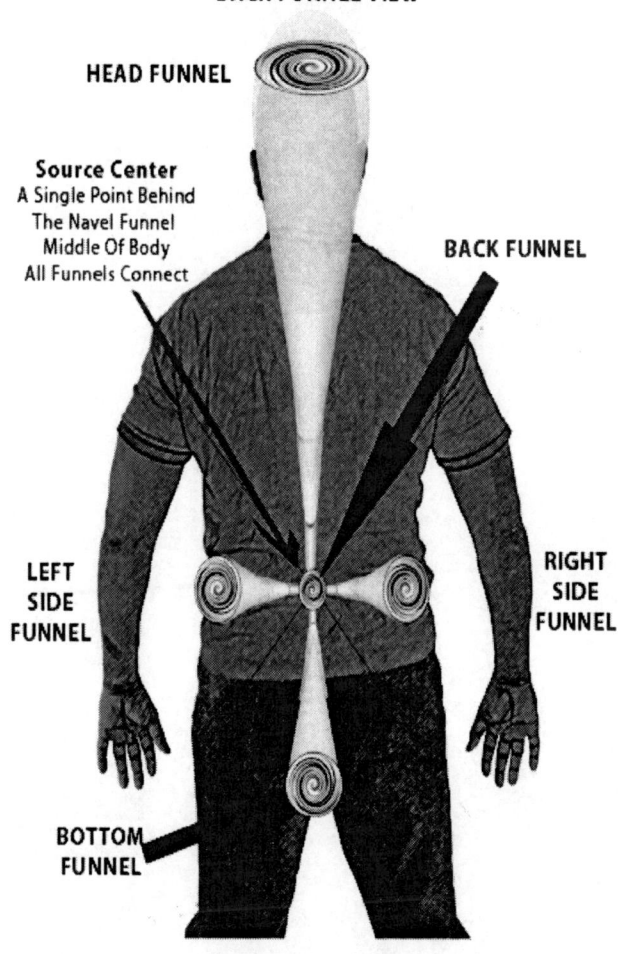

Illustration (E.3)

www.GodsLoveandLight.com/higherlearning

BREATHE IN GOD'S LOVE AND LIGHT AND MANIFEST YOUR DREAMS

BY WALTER BECKLEY

BREATHE IN GOD'S LOVE AND LIGHT AND MANIFEST YOUR DREAMS

BY WALTER BECKLEY

MANIFESTING YOUR DREAMS

BREATHE IN GOD'S LOVE AND LIGHT AND MANIFEST YOUR DREAMS

BY WALTER BECKLEY

MANIFESTING YOUR DREAMS
Advanced Instructions

Below you will find a list of key Focus Power Breathing affirmations for designing and manifesting your life's dreams. After cultivating your inner awareness with God's Love and Light for at least 45 to 60 days, you are now ready to start inserting Love and Light around the various aspects of your life. You can use any of the following affirmations. Feel as if you are inhaling the positive quality of the affirmation into your body and into your life.

While you are cultivating an affirmation, feel a sense of warmth as you smile and focus power breathe that quality into your navel center. It is important to feel a sense of expansion in the naval center as you inhale and contraction in the abdomen in as you exhale.

Choose one and nurture the essence of that quality for seven days.

1. Inhale Love and Light and Abundance into your source center
2. Inhale Love and Light and Health into your source center

BREATHE IN GOD'S LOVE AND LIGHT AND MANIFEST YOUR DREAMS

BY WALTER BECKLEY

3. Inhale Love and Light and Wealth into your source center
4. Inhale Love and Light and Perfect Relationships into your source center
5. Inhale Love and Light and Giving To Others into your source center
6. Inhale Love and Light and Being of Service into your source center
7. Inhale Love and Light and Mental Clarity into your source l center
8. Inhale Love and Light and Emotional Release into your source center
9. Inhale Love and Light and Forgiveness into your source l center
10. Inhale Love and Light and the Willingness to Change into your source center
11. Inhale Love and Light and Transformation into your source center
12. Inhale Love and Light and Personal Growth into your source center
13. Inhale Love and Light and Emotional Growth into your source center
14. Inhale Love and Light and Spiritual Growth into your source center

CONCLUSION

In conclusion, only you have command over the direction your life takes. This is based on what you decide to cultivate, both consciously and unconsciously. It is important to understand that even at this very moment, you are receiving all that you have ever desired; no matter how convoluted it may seem to you. This is due to the combination of thoughts and desires that you carry within you. By cultivating God's Love and Light, you start to burn through your massive graveyard of negative emotional creations. Although many students have had very powerful experiences the very first time, give yourself 90 days to practice and cultivate God's Love and Light in your life, and you will begin to experience the positive difference.

This book and its lessons are designed to assist you in cracking the ultimate code – about your life as you stand in relationship with God's Love and Light. His healing power offers you accessibility to optimal health, enlightened wealth, prosperity, harmonious relationships, careers, and spiritual salvation. In essence all that you need can be found within the power and Glory of God's Love and Light. Why are you weeping and living outside of your true potential? Your claim on the Holy Spirit is only a breath away! It is time to experience the glory of God in your life here on earth, right here and now.

BREATHE IN GOD'S LOVE AND LIGHT AND MANIFEST YOUR DREAMS

BY WALTER BECKLEY

The cultivation of God's Love and Light in your life will transform you and give you all that you desire. A kaleidoscope of unimaginable beauty waits within you. Although this book is an introduction to your inner life experience with God, the real power comes as you learn to spend consistent time cultivating your inner garden of Love and Light. This information is very much like learning a new language. Children usually learn new languages much easier than adults. And so it is with this training; it is a new way to communicate with the Creator and with one another, in love. Be like children, like Jesus said! Enjoy your time, steal away and go within. Play in your garden of Love and Light until your outer world mirrors the Love and Light that comes from the Creator.

In Chapter 9, we looked at opening and activating God's Love and Light in your life through the Focus Power Breathing Method. This process goes much deeper than reading and or confessing what you want in life. In chapter 9 we went into the actual method - the nuts and bolts of 'how to' and 'why'. The power is not in reading or listening to others talk about God, it is in the personal communication or relationship beyond your limited thinking and warped expressions. Drop your babble and

BREATHE IN GOD'S LOVE AND LIGHT AND MANIFEST YOUR DREAMS

BY WALTER BECKLEY

become still; lose yourself in Divine union with the Creator; and become as one, lost in God's Love and Light.

It is my wish and prayer that the power of God's Love and Light blesses you always and directs you towards unlimited peace, dynamic grace, and love.

In God's Love and Light,

Walter L. Beckley

BREATHE IN GOD'S LOVE AND LIGHT AND MANIFEST YOUR DREAMS

BY WALTER BECKLEY

ABOUT THE AUTHOR

For over 30 years, Walter Beckley has trained in various life empowering, healing and awakening modalities. His intense desire to expand and transform his own life has enabled him to assist and motivate others to expand and uncover their own creative power, inner beauty and passion.

Walter has traveled, studied and taught in the USA, India, Thailand, Mexico, Brazil, and the Caribbean.

Walter is certified in various forms of Chi Kung (energy exercises), Taoist forms of Meditation and Relaxation, Korean Hand Acupuncture, Relationship and Addiction Counseling, Chi Nei-Tsang, (internal organ massage).

BREATHE IN GOD'S LOVE AND LIGHT AND MANIFEST YOUR DREAMS

BY WALTER BECKLEY

CLASSES, PRODUCTS, AND CONTACT

To further enhance your knowledge and experience of God's love in life, I set up a membership site where you can communicate with me and others like you, who are learning to cultivate their relationship with God's Love and Light.

On this unique site you can access basic material as well as information about various levels of advanced training. You will also find dates for seminars, interactive telephone and conference calls, and webinars. Products such as the Ocean Breathing musical training CD and the Focus Power Personal Development CD's and DVDs, are available at: http://www.GodsLoveandLight.com/higherlearning site.

I look forward to hearing about your progress and answering your questions as you journey and develop your relationship with God's Love and Light.

If you have questions or comments, please contact me at: contact@GodsLoveandLight.com

With warmth in God's Love and Light,

Walter L. Beckley

BREATHE IN GOD'S LOVE AND LIGHT AND MANIFEST YOUR DREAMS

BY WALTER BECKLEY

RESOURCE CENTER

For a more in-depth connection and understanding, be sure to visit our website and learn more about our other products and services.

Be sure to join our telephone conference calls, webinars, and live 2, 3, 7 & 30 day intensives.

www.GodsLoveandLight.com/higherlearning

Group and Private Classes are Available.

contact@GodsLoveandLight.com

BREATHE IN GOD'S LOVE AND LIGHT AND MANIFEST YOUR DREAMS

BY WALTER BECKLEY

MAY YOU ALWAYS BE IN THE PRESENCE AND ESSENCE OF GOD'S LOVE AND LIGHT

WALTER L. BECKLEY

BREATHE IN GOD'S LOVE AND LIGHT AND MANIFEST YOUR DREAMS

BY WALTER BECKLEY

NOTES

BREATHE IN GOD'S LOVE AND LIGHT AND MANIFEST YOUR DREAMS

BY WALTER BECKLEY

NOTES